One Pot Cookbook

"One-Pot Harmony: Simplicity, Flavor, and Effortless Culinary Joy"

By Daniel Jhons

© Copyright 2025 - All rights reserved.

Table of Contents

Introduction

The mere idea of putting together a scrumptious and nutritious lunch can appear to be an insurmountable obstacle when we consider the pace at which we typically live our lives. When we are burdened by the responsibilities of work, family, and innumerable other commitments, our kitchens become into a battlefield of competing priorities, and the idea of preparing a meal at home can easily fall through the cracks as a result.

Take a look at this: You get home from a long, exhausting day with a mind full with responsibilities and due dates for work. The last thing you want to do is spend hours toiling away in the kitchen, juggling various pots and pans, only to be met with a mountain of filthy dishes later. The struggle is real, and it is an experience shared by numerous people on a daily basis. It is also a worldwide phenomenon. I really get it because I've been in the same situation.

But what if I told you that there is a gastronomic haven that is eagerly awaiting your arrival to save you from the chaos? A place where the art of cooking is stripped of superfluous complications, where the answer rests in the magic of a single pot, and where simplicity and flavor coexist in perfect harmony. We would like to take this opportunity to welcome you to the world of the "One-Pot

Cookbook," which will serve as your culinary guide to preparing delicious and simple meals without the stress of a crowded kitchen.

In the pages that are to come, I will lead you on a journey through the world of cuisine where the symphony of tastes does not require a cacophony of kitchenware. This is not merely a cookbook; rather, it is your ticket to regaining the joy of cooking while also reducing the stress associated with the activity. Imagine the pleasure of savoring rich, substantial soups, delighting in delectable pastas, and relishing the aroma of perfectly seasoned rice—all from the convenience of a single pot. This is exactly what you can do. You are at the vanguard of this gastronomic revolution that is currently taking place.

Why should you take the plunge into the realm of cooking using only one pot? because your time is valuable and your health should come before everything else in importance. This book is not merely a collection of recipes; rather, it is a savior for harried people who are looking for peace and quiet in the kitchen. You may make meals that are worthy of a gourmet restaurant with very little work and experience a great deal of satisfaction with just one pot. It's the most important cooking tip that you'll ever receive, and it will fundamentally alter the way you approach the kitchen.

You will learn the skill of producing soups that warm the spirit, pasta dishes that excite the taste buds, and casseroles that redefine what it means to be comfortable as you make your way through this gourmet trip. Put an end to the confusion caused by multitasking and welcome the simplicity of using just one pot. This is not a concession; rather, it is a revelation—a gastronomic awakening that will rethink how you approach mealtimes in the future.

You may be thinking at this point, "Why should I believe the guidance contained inside these pages?" I see your point. Permit me to reassure you that I am not simply a chef or a food enthusiast; rather, I am your culinary confidant and a fellow warrior in the fight for meals that are both well-balanced and fulfilling. The solutions presented in this book are the product of experience, trial and error, and yes, even a few failed attempts. I have personal experience with the challenges, so I can empathize with readers.

Believe me when I say that this is the perfect book for someone like you. The "One-Pot Cookbook" is your friend whether you're just starting out in the kitchen or you're a seasoned home cook looking for a break from the mayhem of the kitchen. It is time to begin the process of reclaiming your kitchen, one pot at a time. Get ready to go on a culinary journey that is not just about meals; rather, it is about reclaiming the joy, simplicity, and satisfaction that can be found in the process of cooking. Your road to stress-free dinners that are scrumptious awaits you as the one-pot revolution gets underway.

The Beauty of One-Pot Cooking

The beauty of one-pot cooking shines through as a beacon of simplicity, efficiency, and flavor in the frantic dance of modern life, where time is a luxury and the kitchen frequently feels like a battlefield. This style to cooking, which entails creating a full dinner in a single saucepan or skillet, is more than just a passing fad; rather, it represents a paradigm shift in the way food is traditionally prepared. Let's get into the nitty-gritty of the one-pot wonder that is cooking and see what all the fuss is about.

1. Effortless Simplicity

Cooking with only one pot exemplifies the spirit of uncomplicatedness. The days of handling many pots and pans while simultaneously coordinating a complex ballet of time and temperatures are long gone. Instead, you place all of the ingredients in a single container and, with the skill of a seasoned chef, you allow the flavors to combine and mingle with one another. The cooking process is simplified, freeing you to concentrate on the pleasure of producing something new rather than the strain of juggling multiple responsibilities at once.

2. Flavor Fusion

The richness of taste that can be achieved with a single pot of food preparation is one of the most alluring features of this method of cooking. Even the simplest of recipes may be elevated to a higher level by producing a symphony of flavor by allowing the components to exchange flavors as they simmer and mix together in the limited space of the pot. This flavor fusion's beauty lies not just in its taste but also in its capacity to convert ordinary items into spectacular culinary experiences. This is what makes it so beautiful.

3. Versatility in Ingredients

Cooking with only one pot presents an opportunity for you to express your creativity. One pot can suit all of your culinary needs, whether you favor meals that are heavy on meat, follow a plant-based lifestyle, or have a craving for the eclectic fusion of cuisines from around the world. Because of this method's adaptability, you can play around with the ingredients and tastes you use, making it possible to engage in exploratory cooking without the anxiety that comes with the potential for a messy aftermath in the kitchen.

4. Time Efficiency

Cooking with only one pot is a time-saving innovation that shines brightest in a society where time is the most valuable resource. Not only does the use of a single pot cut down on the amount of time needed for preparation and cleanup, but it also makes it possible to cook food more slowly and for longer periods of time, which can result in an increase in flavor intensity. It is the pinnacle of productivity without compromising the high quality of the dishes that you produce in the kitchen.

5. Nutrient Preservation

The beauty of cooking with only one pot extends beyond the benefits of ease and flavor to include the ways in which it helps to retain nutrients. One-pot cooking, as opposed to cooking methods that include several cooking vessels and may result in the loss of nutrients during the process, frequently involves simmering or slow-cooking, both of which help to preserve the nutritional value of the food.

Benefits of One-Pot Meals

Now that we've discussed the aesthetic value of one-pot meals, let's shift our attention to the practical advantages that these meals bring to the table, both in a literal and figurative sense. The benefits of adopting this method to cooking are extremely diverse, ranging from positive effects for one's health to financial savings, and the recipes themselves are just as diverse.

1. Minimal Cleanup

The first advantage of one-pot meals, and possibly the one that receives the most attention, is that they require very little cleaning. You now just have one pot to clean, rather than the pile of dirty dishes and utensils that you normally have to deal with. This not only helps save time, but it also makes the cooking process more accessible to people who might otherwise be put off by the idea of having to clean up after themselves for an extended period of time.

2. Cost-Effective Cooking

One-pot recipes frequently make use of uncomplicated and inexpensive materials. This not only makes them approachable, but it also makes them economical, which is very helpful for people who are conscious of the amount they spend on groceries. It is possible to prepare filling meals without blowing your budget if you make use of foods that are versatile and essential cupboard items.

3. Healthier Eating Habits

Meals that only require one pot are one approach for people who are health conscious to adopt healthy eating behaviors. The contained environment of a single pot enables accurate portion sizes and the uncomplicated monitoring of ingredients, which in turn promotes meals that are nutritionally sound and well-balanced. In addition, the emphasis placed on using fresh, unprocessed ingredients in the preparation of many one-pot meals is consistent with an approach to nutrition that is holistic.

4. Flavor Intensification

The flavors become more intense as the components cook together in the confined space of a single pot, which results in the creation of rich and nuanced flavor profiles. Those individuals who are looking for gastronomic delight without relying on an excessive amount of fats or salts will find that this flavor concentration is a godsend. Cooking in a single pot demonstrates that a greater complexity of flavor may be achieved via the use of natural processes and the interaction of ingredients.

5. Time Efficiency: A Repeat Benefit

Although saving time was emphasized when discussing the allure of cooking with a single pot, this advantage deserves to be brought up on its own as a separate perk. The time savings are not limited to the kitchen; because there is less time spent on meal preparation, there is more time available for other elements of life, such as work, family, or personal activities. Meals that only require one pot to prepare are a culinary ally in the fight for a healthier and more productive way of living.

Essential Tools and Ingredients

To ensure that your adventure in one-pot cooking is a fruitful one, it is essential that you come prepared with the necessary equipment and supplies. Let's take a look at the fundamentals that are required to transform your kitchen into a one-pot wonderland.

Tools

1. Quality Dutch Oven or Casserole Dish

The key to successful one-pot cooking is having a high-quality Dutch oven or a casserole dish that can be used for a variety of purposes. Because of their thick bottoms and their ability to hold heat, these pots and pans are perfect for low and slow cooking methods such as braising, simmering, and braising. These methods result in better flavor development and more even heat distribution.

2. Non-Stick Skillet or Saute Pan

A saute pan or skillet that doesn't stick to food is an absolute necessity for any recipe that calls for rapid sautéing or stir-frying. To ensure that the food is cooked evenly, look for a pan that has a handle that is well made and is good at retaining heat.

3. Slow Cooker or Instant Pot

Even though they are not technically pots, a slow cooker and an Instant Pot can be indispensable tools for one-pot cooking. Because of its capacity to cook food either slowly over a long period of time or quickly under pressure, pressure cookers bring up a wide variety of creative possibilities for producing tasty and delicate dishes.

4. Sharp Chef's Knife

Chopping, dicing, and slicing are all tasks that benefit from having a chef's knife that is both trustworthy and razor sharp. A high-quality knife makes the process of preparing one-pot meals much easier by streamlining the preparation work that is required.

5. Wooden Spoon or Silicone Spatula

The processes of stirring and mixing are essential to cooking with only one pot, and using a wooden spoon or a silicone spatula protects the surfaces of your pots and pans from being scratched or marred in the process.

Ingredients

Now, let's have a look at the fundamental components that support one-pot cooking and make it possible for you to invent a broad variety of tasty recipes. One-pot cooking is a cooking method in which all of the ingredients are prepared in the same pot.

1. Aromatic Vegetables: Onions, Garlic, and More

Numerous one-pot dishes get their distinctive flavor from a flavor basis that consists of the aromatic trinity of onions, garlic, and frequently celery and carrots. These components provide dishes an additional layer of nuance and complexity, giving a solid groundwork for your original culinary creations.

2. Versatile Proteins: Chicken, Beef, or Legumes

Choose proteins that can withstand extended cooking times so that they can infuse flavor into your recipes. This will bring out the meat's natural flavor. For dishes that just require one pot, some fantastic options include chicken thighs, beef stew meat, or robust legumes like lentils.

3. Broths and Stocks

Many one-pot dishes rely on a tasty broth or stock as their liquid foundation because of its versatility and ease of preparation. The flavor profile of your dishes can be improved by using a broth of superior quality, regardless of whether the broth is made from chicken, beef, or vegetables.

4. Grains: Rice, Pasta, and Quinoa

Include grains like rice, pasta, or quinoa in your one-pot meals so that they have more substance and fill you up. These components take on the flavor of whatever they're combined with and contribute to the dish's overall pleasant texture.

5. Fresh Herbs and Spices

Elevate your one-pot creations with a selection of fresh herbs and spices. Whether it's the freshness of cilantro, the warmth of cinnamon, or the kick of cayenne, these elements add layers of flavor and complexity.

6. Vegetables: The More, the Merrier

Include a variety of colorful veggies in your one-pot dinners to boost the nutritional content and aesthetic appeal of these simple dishes. Your culinary creativity is the only thing that can limit the range of veggies available to you, which includes anything from bell peppers and zucchini to leafy greens and tomatoes.

7. Liquids: Wine, Vinegar, and More

You may give your dishes more dimension and character by adding a splash of wine, drizzling on some vinegar, or even squeezing on some citrus. These liquids not only contribute to a flavor that is complete but also deglaze the pan, thereby retrieving delectable morsels that have adhered to the bottom of the pan.

8. Cheese and Cream

Some one-pot recipes could benefit from the addition of cheese or cream in order to get a more decadent and luxurious end result. These components have the potential to take your recipes to the next level, whether you're making a cheesy casserole or a silky risotto.

The capacity to simplify, improve, and entirely revamp one's experience of cooking is what makes cooking in a single pot one of the most attractive aspects of this method. One-pot dinners provide a harmonic approach to cooking that is appealing to both inexperienced cooks and experienced chefs for a variety of reasons, including the practical benefits of saving time and having less cleanup to do and the aesthetic attraction of taste fusion.

It is important to keep in mind that transitioning to one-pot cooking requires more than simply a change in cooking method; it also requires a change in mentality. Remember this as you begin your adventure into one-pot cooking, armed with the appropriate tools and supplies. Embrace the straightforwardness, savor the flavors, and revel in the pleasure of preparing meals that not only satiate the body's nutritional needs but also calm the spirit. It's not just the recipes themselves that make one-pot cooking so appealing; it's also the way in which it elevates the mundane process of cooking into an art form, turning it into a celebration of delicious food, time spent with loved ones, and the satisfaction of a thoughtfully prepared dinner.

Ensuring a Safe Culinary Haven

The kitchen, which is frequently referred to as the "heart" of the home, is a location where inventiveness, sustenance, and friendship all come together. On the other hand, it is also home to a number of possible dangers that have the ability to transform an enjoyable culinary experience into a hazardous one. Safety in the kitchen is of the utmost importance, and it transcends the bounds of one's level of culinary expertise. This is done to protect against accidents and to foster an environment that is safe for cooks of all levels of experience. In this extensive book, we will investigate the diverse world of kitchen safety, discussing the various dangers, providing preventative methods, and cultivating a culture that values culinary wellness.

Understanding Kitchen Hazards

1. Slips, Trips, and Falls

The floor in the kitchen, which is frequently exposed to spills and splatters, can rapidly turn into a potentially hazardous area. Slips, stumbles, and falls brought on by liquids, oils, or food particles that have fallen to the floor can result in injuries ranging from minor bruising to catastrophic fractures.

Preventive Measures:

Promptly clean up spills.

Use slip-resistant mats near sinks and workstations.

Keep floors dry and well-maintained.

2. Burns and Scalds

Burns and scalds are an ever-present danger in the kitchen due to the presence of hot surfaces, liquids that are boiling, and cookware that are sizzling. These wounds can range from relatively minor to life-threatening, and they all require rapid attention and, in the most serious situations, medical attention.

Preventive Measures:

Use oven mitts or potholders when handling hot cookware.

Turn pot handles inward to prevent accidental knocks.

Be cautious around steam and hot surfaces.

3. Cuts and Lacerations

In spite of the fact that they are indispensable in the kitchen, sharp kitchen implements like knives, slicers, and graters provide a high danger of cuts and lacerations. Accidents can occur in the kitchen if food is not handled properly or if the cook is not paying attention to what they are doing.

Preventive Measures:

Keep knives sharp; dull knives can be more dangerous.

Use cutting boards to provide a stable surface.

Pay full attention to the task at hand when using sharp utensils.

4. Electrical Hazards

The kitchen is home to a plethora of different kinds of electrical appliances, ranging from food processors and toasters to ovens and microwaves. Electrical shocks and fires are both possible outcomes of faulty or improperly used electrical equipment, as well as damaged cords.

Preventive Measures:

Regularly inspect cords for fraying or damage.

Unplug appliances when not in use.

Avoid overloading electrical outlets.

5. Choking and Inhalation Risks

Consuming small food items, especially when you are a child, can put you at risk of choking. Inhaling the fumes that are produced when food or cleaning products are burned might also have negative consequences on one's health.

Preventive Measures:

Cut food into small, manageable pieces.

Store cleaning agents properly and use in well-ventilated areas.

Keep the kitchen well-lit to avoid confusion with similarly colored items.

Creating a Safety-Conscious Kitchen Environment

1. Organized Workspace

Keeping the kitchen neat and tidy is one of the most important aspects of food preparation safety. Not only does an area that is devoid of clutter make the process of cooking more efficient, but it also lowers the possibility of injuries occurring. Create a workplace that is organized and productive by assigning distinct locations for various items, such as utensils, cutting boards, and appliances.

2. Proper Handling and Storage of Utensils

It is absolutely necessary to properly store and handle cooking equipment in order to reduce the risk of cuts and other accidents. To prevent unnecessary reaching and potential spillage, utensils with handles ought to be kept within easy reach, while knives ought to be put in blocks that are specifically designed for that purpose or on magnetic strips.

3. Regular Appliance Maintenance

It is essential to do routine inspections and maintenance on kitchen equipment in order to reduce the risk of electrical risks. Check the condition of the cables, make sure they are properly grounded, and promptly replace or repair any piece of equipment that isn't working properly.

4. Safe Food Handling Practices

In the kitchen, ensuring that food is safe to eat is of the utmost importance. Foodborne infections can be avoided to some degree by adhering to appropriate practices for the handling of food. To ensure that meals are both safe and nutritious, it is important to wash one's hands properly before handling food, keep raw and cooked ingredients separate, and adhere to the prescribed temperatures for cooking.

5. Fire Safety Preparedness

It is imperative that the kitchen be outfitted with fundamental fire safety measures. Make sure that there is a fire extinguisher within easy reach, become familiar with how it should be used, and make sure to check the expiration date on it on a regular basis. Additionally, a smoke detector should be placed in or close to the kitchen in order to serve as an early warning system in the event of a fire.

Cultivating a Safety Culture in the Kitchen

1. Educational Initiatives

In the fight against potential dangers in the kitchen, knowledge is your best weapon. Introduce instructional programs into your household or among your culinary crew, putting an emphasis on the significance of maintaining a safe working environment in the kitchen. This can include training courses on the proper handling of knives, awareness of potential hazards, and the protocols to follow in the event of an emergency.

2. Open Communication

Create a setting where people feel comfortable talking about their safety concerns. Establishing a climate in which everyone feels at ease reporting potential dangers, whether it be a malfunctioning appliance, a slippery floor, or a cord that has become frayed, is an important step in developing a proactive safety culture.

3. Emergency Response Planning

Establishing defined emergency response rules will prepare you for any unanticipated scenarios that may arise. Make sure that every member of the family or the staff working in the kitchen is aware of the location of the fire extinguishers, emergency exits, and first aid kits. To improve your level of preparedness, you should hold regular drills.

4. Regular Safety Audits

Conduct routine inspections to ensure the safety of your cooking area. This entails conducting thorough examinations of various appliances, looking for potential dangers, and assessing the level of protection provided by the surrounding environment. Take immediate action to resolve any problems that are discovered during these audits.

Safety is something that should always be kept in mind when venturing into the world of culinary experimentation. The beauty of the kitchen is not only in its potential to conjure delectable dishes, but also in its ability to nurture a safe and nurturing environment for chefs of all levels. This is where the beauty of the kitchen lies. The kitchen can be transformed into a safe haven when potential dangers are recognized, preventative measures are put into place, and a culture of safety consciousness is cultivated. This creates an environment in which the pleasure of cooking can coexist in peace with the knowledge that one is healthy. This will ensure that each dish you prepare is not only a pleasure for the taste buds, but also a demonstration of your dedication to having a safe and pleasurable time in the kitchen.

Breakfast Recipes

1. Cinnamon-Banana Oatmeal

- Serves 8

Ingredients

- 200g gluten-free oats
- 10 ml cinnamon powder
- 4 medium-sized bananas, hashed
- 60g brown sugar
- 60g butter, melted
- 240 ml milk
- 2.5 ml salt

Instructions

1. Put the brown sugar, the butter, and the milk into the slow cooker's saucepan.
2. Prepare on a setting that provides a modest level of heat for one hour.
3. Banana slices, cinnamon powder, oats that are gluten-free, and salt should all be added to the dish.
4. Maintain the cooking temperature for the following 5 hours.
5. Just before serving, dust with a tiny bit more cinnamon than is necessary.

Nutrition: Calories 168, Fat 2.8 g, Carbs 31 g, Protein 6.7 g

2. Blueberry Banana Steel Cut Oats

- Serves 4

Ingredients

- 200g steel-cut oats
- 2 ripe bananas, hashed or mashed
- 150–300g fresh or frozen blueberries
- 480 ml water
- 480 ml milk (almond milk works very well in this recipe)
- 30 ml honey or pure maple syrup
- 1.25 ml salt
- 5 ml cinnamon
- 10 ml vanilla
- Optional add-ins: hashed nuts, nut butter, fresh or dried fruit, granola, shredded coconut, honey, additional milk

Instructions

1. Spraying your slow cooker with non-stick cooking spray will prevent food from adhering to the bottom.
6. Put all of the ingredients into the slow cooker pot and mix them together completely to start the cooking process.
7. You have the option of cooking it on high for two to three hours, or you can cook it on low for six to eight hours throughout the course of the night.

Nutrition: Calories 297, Fat 4.4 g, Carbs 58 g, Protein 8 g

3. Pocket Bacon Breakfast

- Serves 4-6

Ingredients

- 450g bacon, diced
- 60g onion, diced
- 2.5 ml fresh garlic, hashed
- 2 tomatoes, diced
- 1 green or red bell pepper, diced
- 60g cheddar cheese, grated
- 60g parmesan cheese, grated
- 6 eggs
- Salt and pepper

Instructions

1. Arrange slices of bacon, onion, garlic, tomatoes, and bell pepper in alternating layers across the bottom of the slow cooker.
8. Cook on a low setting for a total of five hours.
9. In a basin, the ingredients of eggs, cheddar cheese, and parmesan cheese are combined before being whisked. After putting the components that have been made in the slow cooker, put this mixture on top of the components and turn the slow cooker on high.
10. Cook on a low setting for an additional five hours after this point.
11. As a seasoning, salt and pepper can be added according to personal preference.

Nutrition: Calories 492, Fat 28.6 g, Carbs 31.4 g, Protein 25 g

4. Quinoa Breakfast

Serves 2

Ingredients

- 90g quinoa
- 360 ml almond milk
- 1 date, hashed
- 30g pepitas (pumpkin seeds)
- 1/2 apple, peeled, cored, and diced
- 15 ml cinnamon
- 2.5 ml nutmeg
- 10 ml vanilla extract
- Pinch of salt

Instructions

1. The contents of the crock pot should be placed inside of the slow cooker.
12. Prepare on the HIGH setting for a whole two hours with the lid on the pot.
13. Cook everything throughout the course of the full overnight period at a temperature that is LOW.
14. Your breakfast will be prepared and ready for you when you wake up in the morning.

Nutrition: Calories 400, Fat 2 g, Carbs 22 g, Protein 7 g

5. Easy Breakfast Pear Bake

- Serves 6

Ingredients

- 6 pears, refrigerated
- 60 ml honey
- 5 ml lemon juice
- 5 ml cinnamon
- 30 ml butter, melted
- 200g granola cereal

Instructions

1. To prepare the interior of the slow cooker, spray it with some cooking spray. To prepare the peaches, peel them and cut them into thin slices.
15. Place all of the ingredients in the dish that comes with the slow cooker, then combine them all.
16. Cook on LOW heat with the lid on for somewhere between 6 and 7 hours.

Nutrition: Calories 296, Fat 11 g, Carbs 46 g, Protein 3 g

6. Yogurt Mango Breakfast Dish

- Serves 2 (store leftovers in the fridge for later)

Ingredients

- 960 ml 2% milk
- 60 ml plain yogurt with live cultures
- 2 mangos, diced
- 15 ml honey
- 1.25 ml cardamom, ground

Instructions

1. After putting the milk in the slow cooker and covering it with the lid, set the slow cooker to the LOW setting and let the milk simmer for two hours.
17. After removing the pan from the heat, stir in the yogurt while the milk is still at a warm temperature.
18. To insulate the cooker, first secure the lid, then wrap a thick towel around the housing component of the cooker and place it on the outside of the appliance.
19. Allow it to sit undisturbed for at least eight hours, preferably the whole night.
20. To prepare the dish for serving, divide the mixture across several individual serving dishes.
21. In a mixing dish, combine the hashed up mango, honey, and cardamom.
22. Put any leftovers in the refrigerator to keep them fresh.

Nutrition: Calories 207, Fat 3.2 g, Carbs 31 g, Protein 9.4 g

7. One-Pot Mediterranean Shakshuka

Ingredients:

- 30 milliliters (ml) olive oil
- 1 onion, finely hashed
- 2 bell peppers, diced
- 3 cloves garlic, hashed
- 1 can (400 grams) crushed tomatoes
- 5 grams cumin
- 5 grams paprika
- 2.5 grams chili flakes (adjust to taste)
- Salt and pepper to taste
- 4-6 large eggs
- Fresh parsley, hashed (for garnish)

Instructions:

1. Heat olive oil in a large skillet over medium heat. Sauté the onion and bell peppers until softened.
2. Add hashed garlic and sauté for an additional min.
3. Pour in the crushed tomatoes, cumin, paprika, chili flakes, salt, and pepper. Simmer for 10-15 mins until the sauce thickens.
4. Make small wells in the sauce and crack the eggs into them. Cover and cook until the eggs are done to your liking.
5. Garnish with fresh parsley and serve with crusty bread.

8. One-Pot Oatmeal with Berries and Almonds

Ingredients:

- 100 grams rolled oats
- 500 milliliters milk (dairy or plant-based)
- 150 grams mixed berries (strawberries, blueberries, raspberries)
- 30 grams hashed almonds
- 15 milliliters honey or maple syrup
- Pinch of salt
- Optional: Greek yogurt for serving

Instructions:

1. Combine rolled oats, milk, mixed berries, hashed almonds, honey (or maple syrup), and a pinch of salt in a saucepan.
2. Bring the mixture to a gentle simmer over medium heat, stirring occasionally.
3. Cook until the oats are tender and the berries burst, usually about 10-12 mins.
4. Serve warm, topped with an extra drizzle of honey (or maple syrup) and a dollop of Greek yogurt if desired.

9. One-Pan Breakfast Burrito Dish

Ingredients:

- 15 milliliters olive oil
- 1 bell pepper, diced
- 1 onion, finely hashed
- 240 milliliters black beans, drained and rinsed
- 160 grams corn kernels
- 5 grams cumin
- 5 grams chili powder
- Salt and pepper to taste
- 4 eggs
- 240 milliliters cherry tomatoes, halved
- Avocado slices (for garnish)
- Fresh cilantro, hashed (for garnish)
- Salsa and sour cream (optional, for serving)

Instructions:

1. Heat olive oil in a large skillet. Sauté bell pepper and onion until softened.
2. Add black beans, corn, cumin, chili powder, salt, and pepper. Cook for 5 mins.
3. Create wells in the mixture and crack eggs into them. Cover and cook until eggs are done to your liking.
4. Top with cherry tomatoes, avocado slices, and fresh cilantro.
5. Serve with salsa and sour cream if desired.

10. One-Pot Banana Nut Quinoa Porridge

Ingredients:

- 185 grams quinoa, rinsed
- 500 milliliters almond milk
- 2 ripe bananas, mashed
- 30 grams hashed walnuts
- 15 milliliters maple syrup
- 5 grams cinnamon
- Pinch of salt
- Banana slices and extra walnuts (for topping)

Instructions:

1. In a saucepan, combine quinoa, almond milk, mashed bananas, hashed walnuts, maple syrup, cinnamon, and a pinch of salt.
2. Bring to a boil, then reduce heat to low. Simmer, covered, for 15-20 mins or until quinoa is cooked and the mixture thickens.
3. Stir occasionally to prevent sticking.
4. Serve warm, topped with banana slices and additional walnuts.

11. One-Pan Veggie and Feta Frittata

Ingredients:

- 6 eggs, beaten
- 120 milliliters milk
- 240 milliliters cherry tomatoes, halved
- 30 grams spinach leaves, hashed
- 60 grams feta cheese, crumbled
- 30 grams red onion, finely hashed
- 15 milliliters olive oil
- Salt and pepper to taste
- Fresh herbs (such as basil or parsley) for garnish

Instructions:

1. Preheat the oven to 375°F (190°C).
2. In an oven-safe skillet, heat olive oil over medium heat. Add cherry tomatoes, spinach, and red onion. Cook until vegetables are slightly softened.
3. In a dish, whisk together eggs, milk, feta, salt, and pepper.
4. Pour the egg mixture over the vegetables in the skillet.
5. Cook on the stove for 2 mins, then transfer the skillet to the preheated oven.
6. Bake for 15-20 mins or until the frittata is set and slightly golden.
7. Garnish with fresh herbs and serve directly from the skillet.

Lunch Recipes

12. One Pot Chicken Rigatoni

- Serves 4

Ingredients

- 30 milliliters extra virgin olive oil
- 450 grams chicken breast, diced
- 2 red peppers, hashed into thin strips
- 800 grams (1 can) crushed tomatoes
- 480 milliliters chicken broth
- 450 grams dry rigatoni
- 10 grams Italian seasoning
- 60 grams Parmesan cheese
- 60 grams butter
- 60 milliliters heavy cream
- Crushed red pepper flakes, optional

Instructions

1. Warm the oil in a Dutch oven with a diameter of 12 inches by placing it over medium heat (approximately 20 briquettes). Brown the chicken breasts, but don't bother about completely cooking them through at this point.
2. After adding the strips of red pepper, sauté them for about two mins, or until they start to become pliable.
3. The crushed tomatoes, rigatoni, chicken broth, and Italian spice should all be added now. Place six briquettes on top of the lid, then cover the pot. Bring it up to a boil, and then continue to cook it for another ten to fifteen mins, until the pasta is done. Check on it on a regular basis and, if necessary, make adjustments to the temperature. If more liquid is required, you can always add some.
4. Take the saucepan off the heat and mix in the cream, butter, and Parmesan cheese until combined. Cover it, and let it sit for five mins at room temperature.
5. Serve with more grated Parmesan cheese and crushed red pepper flakes, according to individual preference.

13. Beef Salsa Macaroni

- Serves 6

Ingredients

- 450 grams extra lean ground beef
- 480 milliliters bottled salsa
- 30 grams taco seasoning mix
- 360 milliliters hot water
- 240 milliliters milk
- 240 grams elbow macaroni
- 225 grams processed cheese food (such as Velveeta®), cubed
- 240 grams shredded cheddar cheese
- 120 grams green onion

Instructions

1. Brown the beef in a Dutch oven with a diameter of 12 inches and a fire of 20 briquettes. Remove and discard any excess grease.
2. The salsa, taco seasoning mix, water, and milk should all be stirred in before the mixture is brought to a boil.
3. After adding the macaroni, give it a toss. Turn the heat down to low, cover the pot, and simmer the mixture for the required amount of time.
4. After adding the cheeses, stir the mixture until the cheeses have melted.
5. To serve, bring to a boil and top with hashed green onion.

14. Mac and Cheese

- Serves 4

Ingredients

At home preparation

- 450 grams elbow macaroni, cooked but firm
- 200 grams sharp cheddar cheese, shredded
- 200 grams white cheddar cheese, shredded
- 100 grams Gruyere cheese, shredded
- 50 grams Parmesan cheese
- 10 grams dry mustard
- 5 grams cinnamon
- 5 grams salt
- 4 grams pepper
- 240 milliliters onion, diced at home and stored in an airtight container

Other ingredients

- 60 grams butter
- 20 grams flour
- 600 milliliters milk
- 1 tomato, hashed

Instructions

1. At home, prepare the pasta in accordance with the Instructions provided on the package for al dente pasta. Place in a container that seals tightly or a plastic bag that can be sealed again. Cut the onion into small dice, then store it in a container that will keep out air. Shred the cheeses and combine them. Place in a container that is airtight or a plastic bag that can be sealed again.
2. When you go to the campsite, get the Dutch oven ready by heating the coals to the appropriate temperature for the size of the oven. Put three quarters of the hot coals on the lid of the Dutch oven and set it atop the Dutch oven itself.

3. After the oven has reached the desired temperature, put the butter inside and allow it to melt. Sauté the onion for three mins, or until it begins to get soft, after adding it to the pan.
4. After adding the flour, whisk the mixture for one to two mins, during which time both the flour and the butter should get somewhat toasted.
5. While doing so, gradually pour in the milk in order to break up any clumps that may have formed. Continue to whisk the sauce for another 5 to 7 mins, until it begins to thicken.
6. When adding the cheeses, do so one cup at a time, making sure that each batch is thoroughly combined and melted before proceeding.
7. In order to season the sauce, dry mustard, cinnamon, salt, and pepper should be used. Mix thoroughly.
8. After adding the macaroni, give everything a thorough spin to coat it. Place a layer of hashed tomatoes onto the dish in the final step.
9. Cooking should be done after one hour with the lid on.

15. Stuffed Bell Peppers

- Serves 6

Ingredients

- 6 large bell peppers, tops off, seeds removed
- 30 milliliters vegetable oil
- 450 grams ground beef
- 4 cloves garlic, hashed
- 7.5 grams allspice
- Salt and pepper to taste
- 400 grams white rice (cooked at home)
- 600 milliliters tomato sauce

Instructions

1. Put the Dutch oven into the embers so that it may get hot.
2. Cook the beef, garlic, salt, and pepper until it is browned in the vegetable oil before adding it.
3. Mix together the tomato sauce and the rice that has already been cooked.
4. Place a dollop of the filling inside each bell pepper once it has been cored. Clean the inside of the oven using paper towel.
5. Place the bell peppers that have been packed in a layer in the Dutch oven and cover. Put some coals on the lid of the container.
6. Bake the peppers for twenty to thirty mins, or until they reach the desired degree of tenderness.
7. Serve, and have fun with it!

16. Chicken Jambalaya

- Serves 6

Ingredients

Vegetables

- 1 large onion, hashed
- 1 green bell pepper, hashed
- 3 stalks celery, hashed
- 2 carrots, scrubbed and hashed
- 3 cloves garlic, hashed

Other ingredients

- 30 milliliters canola oil
- 680 grams boneless, skinless chicken, diced
- Salt and pepper to taste
- 400 grams long grain rice
- 15 grams Cajun seasoning
- 720 milliliters water
- 425 grams (1 can) diced tomatoes, with their juices
- 15 grams hashed fresh parsley, for garnish

Instructions

1. At home, clean and cut up the vegetables, then arrange them in a bag that can be sealed back up again.
2. Put 22 briquettes under a Dutch oven measuring 14 inches in diameter. Prepare the chicken by browning it in the hot oil. Add little salt and pepper before serving.
3. After stirring them in, simmer the vegetables for about five mins, or until they start to sweat. After stirring in the rice, continue cooking for an additional five mins, or until the rice develops a light golden color. Do not let it go out in flames.
4. Mix in the tomatoes, chicken broth, and Cajun seasoning, then set aside. Give it a good stir to break up any browned bits of beef that have settled to the bottom of the pan.
5. Set the briquettes up so that eight are on the bottom and twenty are on the top.

Enchilada Casserole

- Serves 6

Ingredients

Spice Mixture:

- 15 grams dried oregano
- 5 grams ground cumin
- 5 grams coriander
- 10 grams onion powder
- 15 grams brown sugar
- 5 grams salt
- 0.25 grams cayenne pepper

Vegetable Packet:

- 1 small onion, diced
- 3 cloves garlic, crushed and hashed
- 1 small red bell pepper, diced
- 1 small green bell pepper, diced

Other ingredients

- 15 milliliters olive oil
- 450 grams chicken breast, hashed
- Salt and pepper to taste
- 425 grams (1 can) crushed or stewed tomatoes
- 720 milliliters chicken broth or water
- 300 grams white rice
- 200 grams canned corn
- 180 grams grated cheddar
- 120 grams green onion, hashed

Instructions

1. At home, create the spice mixture and place it in a small container with a lid or a resealable bag. Bring it with you when you go. After they have been prepared, place the vegetables in a bag that can be sealed again.

2. Put 22 briquettes under a Dutch oven measuring 14 inches in diameter. Prepare the chicken by browning it in the hot oil. Add little salt and pepper before serving.
3. After stirring in the spices and veggies, continue cooking for about five mins, or until the vegetables start to sweat.
4. To the rice, add the tomatoes, as well as the broth or water. Bring the mixture up to a simmer before serving.
5. Place eight briquettes on the bottom and twenty on the top of the stack you just created. Simmer the rice over low heat until it has completely absorbed all of the liquid and is soft, stirring it frequently and adding more liquid if the recipe calls for it.
6. Mix in the corn, then let it to heat up completely. Cheese and green onion should be sprinkled on top before serving.

17. Chicken Rice with Veggies

- Serves 4

Ingredients

- 900 grams large chicken breasts, skinless, cut into chunks
- 30 grams chicken or poultry rub of choice
- 60 milliliters olive oil, divided
- 160 grams (1 package) rice mix (like Knorr or McCormick)
- 480 milliliters water
- Salt and pepper, to taste
- 340 grams (1 bag) mixed veggies, cut into bite-size pieces
- Grated Parmesan cheese, for sprinkling

Instructions

1. The chicken should be seasoned with poultry rub.
2. In a Dutch oven, warm 2 tablespoons of oil by placing it over hot coals or on a burner.
3. After around ten mins, add the chicken chunks and simmer until they become opaque.
4. The chicken should now be placed on a plate.
5. The Dutch oven should now have the remaining oil, water, rice mixture, salt, and pepper. Stir.
6. Cover the pot and reduce the heat to low, allowing it to simmer for up to one min less than the amount of time advised for cooking the rice mix.
7. Take the cover off, and mix in the chicken and vegetables.
8. Replace the lid, and continue to cook over low heat for about 5 to 8 mins, or until the rice has absorbed the majority of the liquid and the vegetables are soft.
9. After serving, cheese should be sprinkled on top.

Creamy Cilantro Chicken and Rice

- Serves 4

Ingredients

- 30 grams butter
- 450 grams boneless, skinless chicken breasts, hashed
- 200 grams uncooked white rice
- 2 cloves garlic, hashed
- 540 milliliters chicken broth or water
- 40 grams loosely packed cilantro leaves, roughly hashed
- 60 milliliters lime juice
- Salt and pepper to taste
- Lime slices, to garnish

For the Sauce

- 1 soft avocado
- Juice of 1 lime
- 60 milliliters milk
- 120 milliliters fresh cilantro, hashed
- 2.5 grams garlic powder
- Salt and pepper to taste

Instructions

1. To melt the butter, use a Dutch oven with a 14-inch diameter over 20 briquettes. The chicken chunks should be browned.
2. Cook for another two to three mins after stirring in the garlic and dried rice. To that, add some water.
3. Bring the mixture to a boil, and while it's boiling, position the briquettes in a stack with eight on the bottom and twenty on the top. Cook for twenty to thirty mins, giving the rice a toss every so often, until the liquid is absorbed and the rice is soft. Mix in the hashed cilantro and lime juice, then season with salt and pepper to taste.
4. In the meantime, get started on the sauce. To obtain a smooth consistency, mash the avocado. Combine the lime juice, milk, cilantro, garlic powder, and seasonings of your choice in a mixing dish. Mix thoroughly with a whisk.
5. The chicken and rice should be served with some of the sauce drizzled over them and some lime wedges.

18. Cowboy Stew

- Serves 4–6

Ingredients

- 450 grams ground beef
- 600 grams potatoes, peeled and diced
- Salt and pepper to taste
- 1 large onion, diced
- 430 grams (1 can) corn, drained
- 430 grams (1 can) peas, drained
- 410 grams (1 can) stewed tomatoes
- 410 grams (1 can) green beans
- 410 grams (1 can) baked beans
- 305 grams (1 can) tomato soup
- 240–480 milliliters water (adjust to desired consistency)
- Salt and pepper to taste

Instructions

1. The steak should be browned in a Dutch oven by placing it over 18–20 briquettes. Remove and discard any excess grease.
2. Stir together after adding the remaining ingredients. Bring it to a low simmer and cook it for the required amount of time for the potatoes to become soft. Salt and pepper can be added to taste as a seasoning.

19. Sweet Potato and Red Lentil Stew

- Serves 4–6

Ingredients

Spice Packet:

- 10 grams chili powder
- 5 grams curry
- 5 grams cumin
- 5 grams turmeric
- 5 grams salt
- 1.25 grams cayenne powder

Vegetable Packet:

- 1 small onion, diced small
- 3 cloves garlic, hashed
- 1/2 - 1 jalapeño, cored and hashed (optional)
- 1 bell pepper, cored and diced

Other Ingredients:

- 30 milliliters coconut or olive oil
- 200 grams red lentils
- 425 grams (1 can) diced tomatoes
- 30 grams tomato paste
- 480 milliliters vegetable broth
- 1 sweet potato, cooked and mashed
- 240 milliliters coconut milk
- 150 grams frozen peas, defrosted

Instructions

1. Preparing the spice and veggie packets at home is the first step. Cook a sweet potato in the oven, then allow it to cool.
2. Put an 18–20 briquette fire underneath a Dutch oven. When the oil is hot, add the vegetables that have been prepped. After five mins of cooking, add the seasonings to the food. Continue to stir and cook for a few more mins.
3. After being thoroughly rinsed, the lentils should be added to the cooking pot together with the tomato cubes, tomato paste, and vegetable stock.

4. Bring the pot to a boil, and then reduce the heat to a simmer and cook the lentils for 15–20 mins, or until they are mushy.
5. Prepare the sweet potato by peeling it and mashing it. Include that in the saucepan, then mix it in thoroughly.
6. Cook until the coconut milk and frozen peas are thoroughly warmed through after adding them.

20. Beef Bourguignon

- Serves 4–6

Ingredients

Vegetable Packet:

- 200 grams carrots, hashed
- 120 grams small pearl onions, peeled
- 225 grams mushrooms, hashed
- 4 cloves garlic, halved

Other Ingredients:

- 150 grams bacon (6 slices)
- 1.36 kilograms stewing beef, cut into bite-sized pieces
- 480 milliliters dry red wine
- 45 grams all-purpose flour
- 480 milliliters beef stock
- 30 grams tomato paste
- 120 milliliters tomato sauce
- 2.5 grams thyme
- 1 bay leaf

Instructions

1. Cook the vegetables in your own kitchen. Before placing the mushrooms in the bag, wrap each one in a separate piece of kitchen towel; this will help prevent the mushrooms from taking in an excessive amount of moisture.
2. Cook the bacon over 22 briquettes in a Dutch oven measuring 14 inches in diameter until it is crispy. Take the bacon out of the pot and set it aside using a slotted spoon.
3. Brown the meat well in the saucepan by adding it in portions and working methodically. While you work, transfer the pieces to a dish, and make sure not to overcrowd the pot.
4. Cook the vegetables in the drippings until they begin to become more pliable after emptying the veggie bag into the drippings. After adding the red wine, give the mixture a

good swirl while scraping the bottom of the saucepan to loosen any browned bits.

5. First, whisk together a little amount of the beef stock and the flour until the mixture is smooth, and then add this mixture to the saucepan along with the remaining liquid, the tomato paste, and the tomato sauce.
6. Reintroduce the beef and bacon to the saucepan, along with the thyme and bay leaf. Stir to combine.
7. Place the briquettes so that there are eight on the bottom and sixteen on the top. Maintain a moderate simmer for the next one and a half hours, stirring occasionally to ensure even cooking.

21. Sausage and Chicken Stew

- Serves 4–6

Ingredients

Spice Packet:

- 5 grams dried oregano
- 5 grams dried basil
- 5 grams dried marjoram
- 2.5 grams crushed red pepper flakes
- 15 grams cornstarch

Vegetables:

- 1 large onion, hashed
- 1 green bell pepper, hashed
- 1 red bell pepper, hashed
- 1 jalapeño, hashed (optional)
- 6 garlic cloves, hashed

Other Ingredients:

- 4–6 mild or spicy Italian sausages
- 5 potatoes, scrubbed and quartered
- 400 grams (1 can) stewed tomatoes
- 170 grams (1 can) tomato paste
- 240 milliliters water
- 100 grams shredded mozzarella cheese

Instructions

1. When you get back to your house, put the spice mixture into a tiny jar that has a cover that fits it tightly. After they have been washed and hashed, the veggies should be placed in a bag that can be sealed.
2. Put a Dutch oven that's 14 inches across on top of 24 briquettes. Cut the chicken and sausage into pieces and brown them. Remove and discard any excess grease.
3. After adding the veggie packet, continue to simmer the vegetables for approximately 5 mins, or until they begin to get softer.

4. Mix in the seasonings along with the rest of the ingredients, EXCEPT for the cheese.
5. Bring the mixture to a low boil, then reduce the heat to a simmer and cook for about 45 mins, or until the flavors have merged and the potatoes are completely cooked.
6. Serve with some mozzarella crumbled on top as a garnish.

22. Hearty Vegetable Stew

- Serves 6–8

Ingredients

For the Base:

- 15 milliliters olive oil
- 1 small onion, hashed
- 1 clove garlic, hashed
- 1 stalk celery, hashed
- 1 small carrot, hashed
- 60 milliliters water

Vegetable Packet

- 1 large onion, diced
- 2 medium carrots, hashed
- 2 ribs celery, hashed
- 3 potatoes, diced
- 225 grams mushrooms, hashed

Other Ingredients:

- 120 milliliters red wine
- 2 potatoes, diced
- 5 grams Italian seasoning
- 960 milliliters low sodium vegetable broth
- 425 grams (1 can) diced tomatoes
- 240 milliliters tomato sauce
- 15 milliliters balsamic vinegar
- 15 grams cornstarch
- Salt and pepper to taste

Instructions

1. When you come back to your house, mince the veggies for the base and put them in a jar that has a lid. Peel and chop the vegetables for the vegetable packet, making sure to wrap the mushrooms in a layer of paper towel to help prevent them from soaking up an excessive amount of moisture while you work.

2. Place a Dutch oven that is 12 inches in diameter over 20 briquettes at the campsite. While the oil is heating, add the veggies for the base along with the water. Cook until the water has evaporated and the veggies have turned a golden color, turning the pan regularly. This contributes to the flavor of the broth that is being made.
3. After adding the wine, make sure to deglaze the pan.
4. Mix in the contents of the vegetable packet, the diced potatoes, the Italian spice, the vegetable broth, the diced tomatoes, and the tomato sauce.
5. Bring the mixture to a boil and then reduce the heat to a simmer for around twenty mins, or until all of the veggies are cooked.
6. Mix the vinegar and cornstarch together, then stir the mixture into the sauce. Salt and pepper can be added to taste after you've had a taste test.

23. Lamb Vindaloo Stew

- Serves 4–6

Ingredients

Lamb Stew Meat:

- 450 grams lamb stew meat, well trimmed and cubed

For the Marinade:

- 2 cloves garlic, crushed
- 1 small onion, hashed
- 2.5 centimeters (1-inch) thumb ginger, hashed
- 2 serrano peppers
- 1 jalapeño pepper
- 5 grams ground cumin
- 5 grams ground turmeric
- 5 grams garam masala
- 5 grams salt
- 2.5 grams ground cloves
- 2.5 grams mustard powder
- 1.25 grams cayenne pepper
- 1.25 grams coriander powder
- 60 milliliters white vinegar

Other Ingredients:

- 30 milliliters coconut oil
- 240 milliliters low-sodium chicken stock
- 120 grams diced fresh tomatoes
- 600 grams medium potatoes, peeled and cubed
- 150 grams frozen carrots and peas mixture
- 120 milliliters coconut milk
- Salt and pepper to taste
- Fresh hashed cilantro, for garnish (optional)
- 400 grams cooked rice, for serving (optional)

Instructions

1. At home, put all of the ingredients for the marinade into a blender or food processor and process them until they form a homogeneous paste.
2. After adding the lamb chunks to a bag that can be sealed, add the marinade to the bag. To ensure that everything is mixed together, carefully manipulate the bag. After putting the bag in the freezer, you should first refrigerate it for four hours.
3. At the campsite, defrost the lamb according to the instructions.
4. Put a Dutch oven that is 12 inches in diameter over 20 briquettes. After the coconut oil has melted, add the lamb along with its marinade and stir to combine. After 5 mins of cooking, add the chicken stock and tomatoes before continuing to cook.
5. The mixture should be brought to a low simmer before the saucepan is covered. Place ten of the briquettes on the bottom and ten more on the top of the stack.
6. Lamb should be cooked for around 15 mins, or until it is tender. Add the potatoes and stir them in. After 15 more mins of cooking, the cover should be replaced.
7. Take off the lid and mix in the carrots, peas, coconut milk, as well as the seasonings of your choice. Cook until everything is hot enough.
8. Serve with rice, and if preferred, garnish with cilantro before serving.

Dinner Recipes

24. Easy Peasy Chicken Alfredo

- Serves 4

Ingredients

- 30 milliliters olive oil
- 680 grams chicken breast, diced
- 3 cloves garlic, hashed
- 240 milliliters milk
- 480 milliliters chicken broth
- 280 grams penne pasta
- 200 grams kale, trimmed and hashed
- 240 milliliters heavy cream
- 120 grams mozzarella, shredded
- 120 grams Parmesan cheese, shredded
- Salt and pepper to taste

Instructions

1. Warm the oil in a Dutch oven by placing it over medium heat (between 18 and 20 briquettes for a pot that is 12 inches in diameter). Cook the chicken breast on all sides until it is browned.
23. After adding the garlic, continue to cook it until it becomes aromatic.
24. The milk and chicken broth should be added, and then the mixture should be brought to a boil. After including the pasta and the kale, cover the pot and then lay six hot briquettes on top of the dish. Maintain a low simmer for 10–15 mins while stirring the mixture occasionally. If more liquid is required, you can add more milk or broth.
25. When the pasta has reached the desired doneness, add the heavy cream, mozzarella, and Parmesan, and toss to combine. To taste, season with salt and pepper, and serve at a warm temperature.

25. Cheesy Penne Pasta in a Pot

- Serves 4

Ingredients

- 30 milliliters olive oil
- 450 grams smoked sausage, thinly hashed
- 125 grams medium onion, hashed
- 2 garlic cloves, finely hashed
- 200 grams mushrooms, hashed
- 280 grams penne pasta, uncooked
- 480 milliliters chicken stock
- 285 grams (1 jar) roasted peppers, undrained
- 200 grams jack cheese, shredded
- 50 grams Parmesan cheese
- 120 grams fresh spinach

Instructions

1. For around ten mins, or until the charcoal briquettes become gray and ashy, light them in a chimney starter. Charcoal should be added to the BBQ pit, and the grate should be positioned in the middle.
2. Olive oil should be heated in a Dutch oven. After adding the onions, let them cook for one to two mins. Include mushrooms, sausage, and garlic in the dish. Sauté the sausages for two to five mins, until they have developed a nice brown color. After that, mix in the pasta, chicken stock, peppers, cheeses, and spinach until everything is well combined. Place a cover over it. After cooking for around 5 to 8 mins, take the cover off the pot. Continue to cook the pasta while stirring it until it reaches the doneness that you choose.
3. After turning off the heat, pour the mixture into a dish for serving.
4. Serve.

26. Tomato Spinach Pasta

- Serves 4–6

Ingredients

- 340 grams dry spaghetti
- 425 grams (1 can) diced tomatoes with liquid
- 1 medium onion, hashed
- 3 cloves garlic, thinly hashed
- 0.25 teaspoons red pepper flakes
- 2 grams dried oregano
- 1065 milliliters vegetable broth
- 30 milliliters extra virgin olive oil
- 150 grams baby spinach
- Parmesan cheese (amount to taste)

Instructions

1. Add all of the ingredients to a Dutch oven that is 12 inches in diameter and place it over 20 hot briquettes. Leave out the spinach and the Parmesan.
2. Bring the pot to a boil, then cover it and add between four and six more briquettes to the top. Allow it to cook for around ten mins, stirring it a few times during the course of the cooking period.
3. Take the pot off the heat as soon as there is approximately an inch of water remaining in the bottom, and then add the spinach. After stirring it, let it sit for a while so the spinach may wilt.
4. Parmesan cheese should be used as a garnish before serving.

27. Dutch Oven Meat Lasagna

- Serves 6-8

Lasagna Noodles:

- 255 grams (1 package) no-boil or oven-ready lasagna noodles

Cheese:

- 450 grams shredded mozzarella
- 50 grams grated Parmesan

Meat Mixture:

- 1/2 medium yellow onion, diced
- 4 cloves garlic, hashed
- 225 grams lean ground beef
- 450 grams Italian sausages
- 2 (680-gram) jars marinara sauce
- 120 milliliters water
- 4 teaspoons sugar
- 2 teaspoons Italian seasoning
- 1 teaspoon dried basil
- 12.5 grams salt
- 2.5 grams black pepper

Ricotta Mixture:

- 450 grams ricotta cheese
- 1 egg, beaten
- 60 milliliters finely hashed parsley
- 5 grams salt

Instructions

1. In your own kitchen, put together the beef mixture. Put the beef, pork sausage, onion, and garlic in a skillet and sauté it over medium-high heat, stirring occasionally, until the meat is browned. The remaining components of the meat

combination should now be added. Maintain a low simmer for half an hour. Refrigerate after storing in a container that can seal out air.

2. In the comfort of your own home, make the ricotta mixture. In a dish, combine all of the ingredients, then transfer the mixture to a container that can seal tightly and place it in the refrigerator.
3. Cheese needs to be made at home. Mix the mozzarella and the parmesan in a dish, then transfer the mixture to a bag that can be sealed and placed in the refrigerator.
4. The lasagna should be put together at the campsite. Prepare a Dutch oven by greasing or spraying it lightly (preferable 12-inch diameter). Begin by laying down a layer of noodles, severing any edges that are too large for the space. Cover with a quarter of the meat mixture. After spreading one-fourth of the ricotta mixture over the meat, sprinkle it with one-fourth of the cheese mixture. Continue piling the ingredients until all of them are used up, finishing with the cheese mixture this time. Make use of broken pieces of spaghetti to fill in the spaces.
5. For a Dutch oven with a diameter of 12 inches, place the oven on around 9–10 hot briquettes and place approximately 15–18 briquettes on the lid. Make the necessary adjustments based on the capacity of your oven.
6. Cook for around forty mins, turning the cover over once every fifteen mins.
7. Take off the heat, and take the cover off the pot.
8. Before serving, let the dish rest for ten mins.

28. Pineapple Fried Rice

- Serves 4

Ingredients

Veggie Bag:

- 1 sweet onion, diced
- 2 stalks celery, diced
- 150 grams cauliflower, hashed to 1.27-centimeter florets
- 150 grams broccoli, hashed to 1.27-centimeter florets
- 100 grams coleslaw mix

Other Ingredients:

- 30 milliliters sesame oil
- 480 grams cooked white rice
- 5 grams sugar
- 15 grams ginger garlic paste
- 30 milliliters soy sauce
- 1 can pineapple tidbits or chunks, drained
- 3 green onions, hashed
- 60 grams cashews, hashed

Instructions

1. Prepare the bag of vegetables and store it in the refrigerator at your house.
2. Warm the sesame oil in a Dutch oven with a diameter of 12 inches by placing it over 18–20 briquettes.
3. After adding the rice, continue cooking for another 5–10 mins while stirring the pot occasionally.
4. The other ingredients, including the contents of the veggie bag, and combine them all in one large dish. Continue to cook for an additional five to ten mins, or until the veggies have become more tender and everything has reached the desired temperature.

Coconut Shrimp with Jerk Rice

- Serves 4-6

Ingredients

- 450 grams shrimp, cleaned and deveined
- 30 milliliters olive oil
- 1 egg, beaten
- Coating Mixture:
- 50 grams unsweetened coconut
- 50 grams panko breadcrumbs
- 80 grams green bell pepper, diced
- 80 grams yellow onion, diced
- 480 grams cooked white rice
- 120 milliliters chicken or vegetable stock
- Spice Mix to Make at Home:
- 5 grams cinnamon
- 2.5 grams allspice
- 5 grams cayenne powder
- 5 grams crushed red pepper flakes
- 10 grams brown sugar
- 5 grams thyme
- 5 grams salt
- 5 grams pepper

Instructions

1. At home, make the seasoning blend and transfer it to a small container with a tight-fitting cover or a bag that can be sealed.
2. To prepare the Dutch oven, heat the coals in a fire pit and then place the oven over the hot coals.
3. After adding the olive oil to the Dutch oven, let it to come to temperature.
4. While everything is going on, combine the shredded coconut and the panko breadcrumbs in a separate dish.

5. After being coated in the beaten egg, each shrimp is then dipped in the coconut mixture and cooked. When the coating has been applied to all of the shrimp, transfer them to the Dutch oven. Before rotating the meat, cook it for two mins.
6. While the shrimp are cooking, put the yellow onion and bell pepper in the skillet. Sauté with a light tossing. Cook the shrimp and vegetables for three to five mins, or until the shrimp are just about ready to be served.
7. Rice and either chicken or vegetable stock should be added to the Dutch oven after the shrimp are moved to the outside edges of the oven.
8. Cinnamon, allspice, cayenne powder, crushed red pepper flakes, brown sugar, thyme, salt, and pepper are the ingredients that make up the spice combination that will be used to season the rice. Continue cooking the rice for another 5 mins, stirring it frequently to ensure that the flavors are well distributed throughout, or until the rice has reached the desired temperature.
9. Place the rice on individual serving dishes, and then place the coconut shrimp on top.

29. Hunter Stew

- Serves 6

Ingredients

Vegetable Packet:

- 1 large onion, hashed
- 3 stalks celery, hashed
- 3 cloves garlic, whole, crushed
- 4 carrots, scrubbed and hashed
- 1 small rutabaga, peeled and cubed

Other Ingredients:

- 680 grams boneless venison (or rabbit, or beef chuck roast), cut in 2.54-centimeter cubes
- 45 milliliters bacon grease
- 1200 milliliters water
- 180 milliliters tomato juice
- 15 milliliters Worcestershire sauce
- 1 bay leaf
- Salt and pepper to taste
- 6 medium potatoes, scrubbed and hashed
- 150 grams peas (frozen and thawed is better than canned)
- 15 grams cornstarch

Instructions

1. At your house, get the onion, celery, and garlic ready, as well as the carrots and rutabaga. Put them in a bag that can be sealed back up again.
2. At the campground, place a Dutch oven that is 14 inches in diameter over 22 briquettes. While the grease from the bacon is heating up, brown the meat nicely.
3. Mix in the tomato juice, Worcestershire sauce, water, and a bay leaf, then season with salt and pepper. Stir vigorously to break up any browned bits that have accumulated on the bottom of the pot.

4. Bring the stew to a boil, and while it's boiling, shift the briquettes so that approximately 18 are on top and 6 are underneath. Make sure that they are always topped off, and stir the stew every once in a while. Allow it to cook at a low simmer for about two hours.
5. Combine the potatoes and the contents of the bag of vegetables and add them to the pot. Simmer the vegetables for the required amount of time.
6. Next, stir in the peas. To thicken the soup, combine the cornstarch with a small bit of water and use this mixture. If preferred, add more salt and pepper to the dish.

30. Italian Chicken Stew

- Serves 4

Ingredients

- 8 chicken thighs, bone-in, skin-on
- Salt and pepper, to taste
- 30-45 milliliters olive oil
- 1 red onion, hashed
- 1 large red bell pepper, hashed
- 3 garlic cloves, finely hashed
- 180 milliliters dry white wine (you could also use chicken stock)
- 800 grams (1 can) crushed tomatoes, with juice
- 225 grams mushrooms, hashed
- 2 bay leaves
- 3 stems fresh thyme

Instructions

1. Use paper towels to thoroughly dry the chicken.
2. Add little salt and pepper before serving.
3. Warm the oil in the Dutch oven set over the coals that have been prepared.
4. After the chicken has been browned on the outside, add it to the pan and sear it on all sides (about 4 mins on each side).
5. Pull the chicken out of the Dutch oven.
6. If more oil is required, add it now.
7. Onion, red bell pepper, and garlic should be cooked until they are soft (about 4 mins).
8. Mix in some smashed tomatoes and wine.
9. Raise the heat to a low simmer.
10. Include the mushrooms and the bay leaves in the dish.
11. Place the chicken breasts back into the Dutch oven.
12. Place a few bits of coal on the lid, then sprinkle the top with thyme.

13. Allow to cook for approximately 30–45 mins, or until chicken is cooked through.
14. Experiment with the flavor, and if necessary, adjust the seasoning with salt and pepper. Before serving, remove and discard the bay leaves and thyme stalks.

31. Garlic Chicken and Veggie Stew

- Serves 6

Ingredients

- 3-4 slices bacon, hashed
- 1.6 kilograms chicken, skinless, cut into about 10–12 pieces
- 1 medium onion, hashed
- 2 stalks celery, hashed
- 1 head garlic, cloves separated and peeled
- 225 grams cremini mushrooms, hashed
- 150 grams frozen pearl onions
- 15 milliliters tomato paste
- 410 grams reduced-sodium chicken broth (1 can)
- 120 milliliters dry white wine
- 225 grams small red potatoes, quartered
- 600 grams medium carrots, cut into bite-size pieces
- 30 grams all-purpose flour
- 30 milliliters water
- Salt and pepper, to taste

Instructions

1. Put the bacon in a Dutch oven and place it over the hot coals.
2. Cook for about four to six mins, or until crisp.
3. Take the food out of the Dutch oven, drain it over some paper towels, and leave it aside.
4. Add salt and pepper to the chicken before cooking. Brown the chicken pieces by searing them in batches for around four to five mins on each side.
5. Put the pieces that have been browned on a plate. Put to the side.
6. The onion, celery, and garlic should be sautéed in the Dutch oven for around two to three mins, or until the edges become slightly browned.

7. To the pan, add tomato paste, pearl onions, and mushrooms. After about 5 mins of stirring, the onions should be aromatic and completely warmed through.
8. To this, add some potatoes, carrots, broth, and wine.
9. Bring the liquid to a boil.
10. Place the chicken and the bacon back into the Dutch oven.
11. Cover and allow simmer for approximately 25 to 30 mins, or until the chicken and veggies are cooked.
12. Flour and water should be mixed together in a cup or a small dish using a whisk to create a smooth paste.
13. Take approximately a quarter cup of the liquid from the Dutch oven and mix it into the paste until you get a smooth consistency.
14. Pour into a Dutch oven and continue to cook over medium heat, stirring frequently, for about ten mins, or until the mixture has thickened.
15. Just before serving, season the food with salt and pepper.

32. Chicken Chili Verde

- Serves 4–6

Ingredients

- 680 grams chicken, cubed
- 15 milliliters olive oil or butter
- 120 grams onion, diced
- 15 milliliters jarred hashed garlic
- 425 grams (1 can) diced tomatoes
- 425 grams (1 can) white northern beans, drained
- 150 grams fresh or frozen corn kernels
- 60 milliliters canned green chilies
- 240 milliliters chicken stock
- 240 milliliters tomato vegetable juice
- 240 milliliters salsa verde
- 5 grams cumin
- 5 grams paprika
- 5 grams salt
- 5 grams pepper

Instructions

1. To prepare the Dutch oven, heat the coals in a fire pit and place the oven on top of the coals once they are hot.
2. After the oven has been preheated, place the chicken, onion, garlic, and olive oil inside. While it is cooking, give it a good toss every 5 mins.
3. The tomatoes, northern beans, corn kernels, and green chilies should all be added at this point. After a thorough mixing, cook for three to five mins.
4. Mix in some vegetable juice, salsa verde, cumin, paprika, and seasonings of your choice, including salt and pepper. Combine thoroughly.
5. Cook the chicken with the cover on for about 40 to 50 mins, or until it is completely cooked through and tender.

33. Beef and Mushroom Rouladen

- Setup: 30mins
- Cook: 2 hours
- Serves: 4

Ingredients:

- 4 beef round steaks, thinly hashed
- Dijon mustard (to taste)
- Season (to taste)
- 8 slices bacon
- 1 huge onion, finely hashed
- 480 grams mushrooms, hashed
- 30 milliliters Oil
- 480 milliliters beef broth
- 240 milliliters red wine
- 30 grams flour
- Fresh parsley

Instructions:

1. Place the beef slices on a plate, and then sprinkle a very thin amount of mustard over each one. Adjust your wardrobe accordingly.
26. Put a slice of bacon on each slice of beef, then add a spoonful of hashed onions and mushrooms to the top of each beef slice.
27. To keep the beef slices in their intended shape, roll them up and secure the rolls with toothpicks.
28. Oil should be heated over moderately high heat in a large skillet. Prepare the beef rolls by browning them on all sides.
29. After it has browned, the rouladen should be transferred to a platter. Put the flour in the same skillet and whisk it constantly to make a roux.
30. To make a smooth sauce, begin by adding beef broth and red wine to the skillet in increments while whisking continuously.

31. Place the beef rolls back into the pan and make sure they are completely covered in the sauce before serving. Keep the lid on and simmer the beef for an hour and a half to two hours, or until it is soft.
32. After it has finished cooking, take out the toothpicks and place the rouladen on a tray ready for serving.
33. If you want the sauce to be thicker, you can do that, and then pour it over the beef rolls.
34. Serve the Beef and Mushroom Rouladen while it is still hot, garnished with fresh parsley, and accompanied by sides such as mashed potatoes or spaetzle.

Nutrition: Kcals: 450 Protein: 30g Carbs: 12g Fat: 28g Fiber: 2g

34. Chicken and Dumplings Bavarian Style

- Setup: 25mins
- Cook: 40mins
- Serves: 6

Ingredients:

For the Chicken:

- 1 whole chicken, cut into parts
- Season to taste
- 30 milliliters Oil
- 1 onion, hashed
- 2 carrots, hashed
- 2 celery stalks, hashed
- 3 cloves garlic, hashed
- 1 bay leaf
- 5 grams thyme, dried
- 1.4 liters chicken broth

For the Dumplings:

- 240 grams flour
- 15 grams baking powder
- 5 grams salt
- 240 milliliters milk
- 30 grams butter, melted
- Fresh parsley

Instructions:

For the Chicken:

1. Use The chicken should be seasoned to taste.
35. To preheat the oil, place it in a large Dutch oven or saucepan and set the heat to medium-high. Make sure both sides of the chicken are browned.
36. Take the chicken out of the pan and put it in a dish of its own away from the heat.

37. While the garlic is being mashed, use the same pan to sauté the carrots, celery, onions, and garlic until the vegetables are soft.
38. After the chicken has been browned, place it back into the pot. Collect the dried thyme, chicken broth, and bay leaf before beginning the recipe.
39. To achieve a tender texture in the chicken, bring all of the ingredients to a boil for a few mins, then reduce the heat, cover, and simmer for forty-five mins to an hour.

For the Dumplings:

40. Whisk the flour, baking soda, and salt together in a dish after combining them in the dish with a whisk.
41. When it appears that the dry ingredients are almost completely incorporated, pour in the milk and whisk in the melted butter. You want the batter to be rather thick.
42. While the chicken stock is simmering, add the batter to it using a spoon, making care to leave an equal amount of space between each mouthful.
43. Put an end to the cooking and let the mixture boil, covered, for fifteen to twenty mins, or until the dumplings are cooked through.

Nutrition: Kcals: 320 Protein: 20g Carbs: 30g Fat: 12g Fiber: 3g

35. Lentil and Vegetable Stew

- Setup: 15mins
- Cook: 1 hour
- Serves: 8

Ingredients:

- 400 grams green or brown lentils, rinsed
- 1 onion, finely hashed
- 2 carrots, hashed
- 2 celery stalks, hashed
- 3 cloves garlic, hashed
- 1 can (400 grams) hashed tomatoes
- 1.4 liters vegetable broth
- 1 bay leaf
- 5 grams cumin, ground
- 5 grams paprika
- Season to taste
- 200 grams kale, hashed
- Fresh parsley

Instructions:

1. Put the lentils, the hashed onion, the hashed carrots, the hashed celery, the hashed garlic, the hashed tomatoes, the vegetable broth, the bay leaf, the ground cumin, the paprika, some salt, and some pepper in a large pot.
44. Bring all of the ingredients to a boil, then reduce the heat to a simmer and cover the pot. The lentils should be cooked until they are soft, which should take anywhere from 45 mins to an hour.
45. The stew will benefit from the inclusion of hashed kale, which should be cooked for an extra ten mins so that the kale can wilt.
46. If necessary, make adjustments to the seasoning, and throw away the bay leaf.

47. The Lentil and Vegetable Stew should be served hot and garnished with fresh parsley before serving.

Nutrition: Kcals: 250 Protein: 15g Carbs: 45g Fat: 2g Fiber: 15g

36. Bavarian Pretzel Dumplings with Beer Cheese Sauce

- Setup: 30mins
- Cook: 25mins
- Serves: 4

Ingredients:

For the Dumplings:

- 4 Bavarian-style soft pretzels, hashed
- 2 eggs
- 120 milliliters milk
- 60 grams fresh parsley, hashed
- Salt and black pepper to taste

For the Beer Cheese Sauce:

- 120 grams sharp cheddar cheese, shredded
- 120 grams Gruyère cheese, shredded
- 15 grams flour
- 240 milliliters German lager beer
- 5 grams Dijon mustard
- 2.5 grams garlic powder
- Salt and cayenne pepper to taste

Instructions:

For the Dumplings:

1. Eggs, milk, hashed parsley, salt, and black pepper should be mixed together in a dish using a whisk.
48. Pretzels that have been crushed should be added to the egg mixture, and you should make sure that they are thoroughly covered.
49. Wait fifteen mins before stirring the mixture again so that the pretzels may fully absorb the liquid.
50. To ensure that the filling is completely cooked through, form the mixture into dumplings and steam them for 20–25 mins.

For the Beer Cheese Sauce:

51. Shredded cheddar, grated Gruyère, and flour should be mixed together in a saucepan set over moderate heat until they form a cohesive mass.
52. While whisking constantly, gradually add the beer, then the Dijon mustard, the garlic powder, the salt, and the cayenne pepper.
53. Keep going until the cheese is completely melted and the sauce has reached the desired consistency.

Nutrition: Kcals: 480 Protein: 22g Carbs: 38g Fat: 25g Fiber: 3g

37. Creamy Chicken Noodles

- Serves: 6-8 Prep Time: 10 mins Cook Time: 35 mins

Ingredients:

- 15 milliliters olive oil
- 450 grams boneless skinless chicken breasts or thighs, cut into 1.27-centimeter pieces
- 7.5 grams salt, divided, plus more as desired
- 0.25 grams black pepper, divided, plus more as desired
- 15 grams butter
- 1 small onion, finely hashed
- 200 grams medium carrots, finely hashed
- 100 grams large celery stalk, finely hashed
- 7.5 grams hashed garlic
- 5 grams fresh thyme
- 900 milliliters chicken broth
- 340 grams egg noodles
- 60 milliliters heavy (whipping) cream, plus 20 milliliters as desired
- 30 grams hashed fresh parsley

Instructions:

1. Turn the temperature in the oven up to 350 degrees Fahrenheit.
2. Warm the olive oil in a Dutch oven over medium-high heat until it shimmers, and then set it aside. After adding the chicken, season it with one teaspoon of salt and one-eighth of a teaspoon of ground black pepper. Five to seven mins of sautéing should result in a very mild browning. Place the chicken on a dinner plate by moving it to the plate with a slotted spoon.
3. Put in the butter, and then wait for it to melt. After adding the onion, carrots, and celery, give everything a good swirl to incorporate everything. Six to seven mins of sautéing should be enough time for the vegetables to become more

tender. After adding the garlic and thyme, continue cooking for about 30 seconds, or until the aroma is released. Stir to incorporate after adding the remaining 12 teaspoon of salt and 1/8 teaspoon of black pepper, along with the chicken stock and the noodles.

4. The liquid should be brought to a boil while the Dutch oven is covered. Once it has reached a boil, reduce the heat to medium-low. After 12 to 14 mins of vigorous simmering, during which time you should toss the mixture a few times, the noodles should be tender and the majority of the liquid should have been absorbed. Take the Dutch oven off the heat and set it aside. Mix together the added parsley, cooked chicken, and a quarter cup of heavy cream until everything is evenly distributed. If you want your dish to have a creamier texture, add an additional four teaspoons of cream.
5. Cover the dish and place it in the oven for about 4 to 5 mins, or until it is heated through. Additional salt and black pepper can be added to taste, and then the dish should be served right away.

Nutrition: Calories: 396; Total fat: 12g; Saturated fat: 5g; Carbohydrates: 44g; Sodium: 664mg; Fiber: 3g; Protein: 26g

38. Barbecue Chicken Skillet Calzone

- Serves: 2 – 4 Prep Time: 10 mins Cook Time: 30 mins

Ingredients:

- Nonstick cooking spray
- 300 grams diced or shredded cooked chicken
- 60 grams shredded mozzarella cheese
- 30 grams shredded Mexican-style cheese blend
- 80 milliliters barbecue sauce
- 30 grams roughly hashed tomato (optional)
- 15 grams roughly hashed red onion (optional)
- 15 grams roughly hashed fresh cilantro (optional)
- 225 grams refrigerated pizza dough

Instructions:

1. Turn the oven temperature up to 400 degrees F. Spray a cast-iron skillet that is 9 inches in diameter with nonstick cooking spray generously.
2. In a large dish, combine the shredded chicken cheese, barbecue sauce, and other shredded cheeses. Mix until everything is well incorporated after adding the tomato, red onion, and cilantro (if using).
3. Roll out the pizza dough into a large rectangle that is roughly 16 inches by 8 inches and just a hair less than a quarter of an inch thick. Place one half of the sheet of dough into the skillet and allow the other half to hang over the edge of the pan. Put the filling into the dough that is already in the skillet, but leave a border of dough around it that is an inch wide. The dough that hangs off the edge should be folded over the filling. To ensure that the calzone is completely sealed, press the bottom and top edges of the dough together and roll them securely inward.
4. Bake for another 25 to 30 mins, or until the crust has a rich golden color and makes a hollow sound when tapped. Halfway through the cooking time, check the crust to see if

it is browning too quickly and cover it loosely with a sheet of aluminum foil if necessary.

5. Wait five mins and then resume. Remove the calzone from the skillet by carefully lifting it using a broad spatula, and then cut it into pieces using a sharp knife. Immediately serve after cooking.

Nutrition: Calories: 633; Total fat: 18g; Saturated fat: 8g; Carbohydrates: 74g; Sodium: 1,306mg; Fiber: 4g; Protein: 43g

39. Turkey Tetrazzini

- Serves: 8 Prep Time: 10 Mins Cook Time: 30 mins

Ingredients:

- 70 grams butter, divided
- 1/2 large onion, finely hashed
- 2 celery stalks, finely hashed
- 200 grams button mushrooms, hashed
- 75 grams frozen peas
- 1.5 teaspoons hashed garlic
- 5 grams salt
- 0.25 grams black pepper
- 180 milliliters white wine
- 780 milliliters whole milk
- 415 milliliters chicken broth
- 450 grams spaghetti
- Nonstick cooking spray
- 180 milliliters heavy (whipping) cream
- 60 grams cream cheese
- 60 grams grated Parmesan cheese
- 450 grams diced or shredded cooked turkey
- 18 buttery round crackers (like Ritz), crushed into crumbs
- Finely hashed fresh parsley, for serving (optional)

Instructions:

1. Butter should be melted into two tablespoons in a Dutch oven set over medium-high heat. After adding the onion, celery, and mushrooms, continue to sauté the mixture for another 6 to 7 mins, or until the mushrooms have shrunk and the onion and celery have become tender. After adding the peas and garlic, continue cooking for another thirty seconds, or until the garlic becomes aromatic. Add some salt and freshly ground black pepper before serving.
2. After adding the white wine, scrape the bottom of the Dutch oven to remove any browned bits that have accumulated

there. After adding the milk, broth, and spaghetti, spritz a few times with a cooking spray designed to prevent sticking. Keep it covered as you bring it to a boil. After the water has come to a boil, turn the heat down to medium-low and continue to simmer the noodles while stirring them frequently until they are soft and the majority of the liquid has been absorbed, which should take between 14 and 16 mins. During the time that the pasta is cooking, adjust a rack in the oven so that it is approximately 12 inches from the source of heat and turn the oven to broil.

3. Take the Dutch oven off the heat and set it aside. After adding the heavy cream, cream cheese, and Parmesan cheese, mix all of the ingredients together until they melt and form a smooth sauce. After incorporating the turkey, scrape the edges of the Dutch oven to ensure even cooking.
4. Put the remaining three tablespoons of butter in a big dish that is safe for the microwave, and melt it in the microwave on high for twenty to thirty seconds, or until it is completely melted. Mix until all of the cracker crumbs are uniformly soaked after adding the crushed crackers. The topping should be distributed evenly over the spaghetti.
5. Place the pot in the oven and broil for approximately two mins while keeping a close eye on it. The topping should be lightly browned and the pasta should bubble slightly around the edges. Immediately serve, garnishing each plate with freshly cut parsley (if using).

Nutrition: Calories: 580; Total fat: 27g; Saturated fat: 15g; Carbohydrates: 57g; Sodium: 632mg; Fiber: 3g; Protein: 23g

40. Louisiana Gumbo

- Serves: 6 – 8 Prep Time: 15 mins Cook Time: 1 hour 10 mins

Ingredients:

- 30 milliliters olive oil
- 15 grams butter
- 30 grams finely hashed bacon
- 400 grams smoked andouille sausage, cut into 0.64-centimeter-thick slices
- 225 grams raw shrimp, peeled
- 150 to 200 grams shredded cooked chicken
- 1 medium onion, diced
- 1 large green bell pepper, diced
- 3 celery stalks, diced
- 10 grams hashed garlic
- 16 grams light or dark brown sugar
- 10 grams paprika
- 4 grams dried thyme
- 3 grams dried oregano
- 2 grams ground mustard
- 1.5 grams ground cayenne pepper
- 2.5 grams salt
- 2.5 grams black pepper
- 60 grams all-purpose flour
- 1.5 liters chicken broth
- 225 grams frozen hashed okra
- 6 scallions, finely hashed
- 60 grams finely hashed fresh parsley
- Cooked rice, for serving

Instructions:

1. Turn the oven up to 350 degrees Fahrenheit.
2. The butter and oil should be warmed in a Dutch oven set over a medium-high heat. After adding the bacon and sausage, continue to sauté the mixture for another 5 to 6

mins, or until the sausage is lightly browned and the bacon is beginning to crisp.

3. After adding the onion, bell pepper, and celery, continue to sauté the ingredients for another three to four mins, or until the veggies have become somewhat softer. After adding the garlic, brown sugar, paprika, thyme, oregano, mustard, cayenne, salt, and black pepper, mix the ingredients by stirring them together. Continue to cook for another min or so, until the aroma becomes fragrant.
4. To coat the meat and veggies, sprinkle the flour over the contents of the Dutch oven and swirl to combine. While stirring constantly, gradually add the broth to dissolve the flour. Cook the broth over medium heat while stirring it regularly for about four to five mins, or until it begins to boil and becomes somewhat thicker. After adding the frozen okra, continue to cook for one to two mins, or until the okra is thawed.
5. Cook the gumbo uncovered in the oven for about 40 to 45 mins, or until the gumbo is bubbling and the vegetables are soft. After removing the shrimp and chicken from the oven, add three quarters of the hashed scallions and parsley, and toss everything together to incorporate. Bake the shrimp for an additional 6 to 7 mins, or until it becomes a pinkish color.
6. Wait at least 15 mins before touching again. On top of the rice, garnish with the remaining scallions and parsley that have been hashed.

Nutrition: Calories: 611; Total fat: 30g; Saturated fat: 10g; Carbohydrates: 53g; Sodium: 990mg; Fiber: 5g; Protein: 33g

41. Easy Camping Chicken Stew

- Serves 4

Ingredients

Prepare at home:

- 1 medium onion, hashed
- 3 stalks celery, hashed
- 3 medium carrots, hashed
- 5 grams dried thyme
- 5 grams dried parsley

Other ingredients

- 680 grams boneless skinless chicken breasts, cut into bite-sized pieces
- Salt and pepper to taste
- 60 grams all-purpose flour
- 45 grams butter
- 200 grams medium potatoes, peeled and cubed
- 240 milliliters chicken broth
- 15 grams cornstarch
- 15 milliliters ketchup

Instructions

1. Prepare the onion, celery, and carrots in your own kitchen by dicing them. Put all of these ingredients, together with the thyme and parsley, into a bag that can be sealed.
2. At the campground, season the chicken breasts with salt and pepper and then coat them in flour. Then, set the chicken breasts aside.
3. Butter should be melted in a Dutch oven that is 12 inches wide and placed over 20 briquettes. After the chicken has developed a lovely brown color, add the potatoes. After a few mins of cooking, add the vegetables that were contained in the bag.
4. Combine the cornstarch and the chicken stock in a separate dish, and then mix both of these ingredients into the pot along with the ketchup

42. Beef and Stout Stew

- Serves 4-6

Ingredients

- 680 grams beef stew meat
- 30 grams butter
- 240 grams yellow onion, diced
- 2 cloves garlic, hashed and crushed
- 120 grams celery, hashed
- 300 grams carrots, hashed
- 400 grams red potatoes, cut into large cubes
- 950-1200 milliliters beef stock
- 355 milliliters stout-style beer
- 15 milliliters tomato paste
- 15 milliliters Worcestershire sauce
- 10 grams mustard
- 5 grams rosemary
- 5 grams paprika
- 15 milliliters honey
- 5 grams salt
- 5 grams pepper

Instructions

1. To prepare your Dutch oven, heat some coals in a fire pit and then place the pot on top of the glowing coals.
2. After the Dutch oven has reached the desired temperature, place the steak, butter, onion, and garlic inside. Turn frequently while cooking for about five mins, or until the meat is browned.
3. Put in the potatoes, along with the carrots and celery. Keep going with the cooking for another three mins.
4. The beef stock, stout beer, tomato paste, Worcestershire sauce, and mustard should be added to the pot. Make sure to stir everything up, then keep it on the stove for another 5 mins.

5. To season, add the honey, paprika, salt, and pepper, as well as the rosemary. Mix thoroughly by stirring.
6. Cook the beef, covered, for about 40 mins, or until it is soft and cooked all the way through.

43. Pioneer Goulash

- Serves 4-6

Ingredients

- 450 grams ground beef
- 240 grams yellow onion, diced
- 120 grams celery, hashed
- 15 milliliters jarred hashed garlic
- 425 grams diced tomatoes
- 425 grams tomato sauce
- 425 grams kidney beans, drained
- 355-360 milliliters water or tomato-based vegetable juice
- 15 milliliters Worcestershire sauce
- 15 milliliters soy sauce
- 5 grams oregano
- 5 grams thyme
- 5 grams paprika
- 5 grams salt
- 5 grams pepper
- 200-400 grams uncooked elbow macaroni (adjust based on preference)

Instructions

1. To prepare the Dutch oven, heat the coals in a fire pit and place the oven on top of the coals once they are hot.
2. Add the ground beef, onion, celery, and garlic once the oven has reached the desired temperature. Turn the meat occasionally while it is cooking for about ten mins, or until it has browned.
3. Mix in the kidney beans, Worcestershire sauce, and soy sauce after you've added the tomatoes and tomato sauce. Cooking should be continued with the lid on until the liquid becomes frothy and heated.
4. Add some oregano, thyme, paprika, salt, and pepper to taste before serving. Keep the heat at a low simmer for another 5 mins.

5. After adding the elbow macaroni, continue cooking, covered, for another 30 mins, or until the macaroni is soft.

Dessert, Soup and Vegetables Recipes

44. Garlic and Herb Spaetzle

- Setup: 20mins
- Cook: 10mins
- Serves: 4

Ingredients:

- 300g flour
- 3 huge eggs
- 150ml milk
- 5g salt
- 30ml unsalted butter
- 2 cloves garlic, hashed
- 30ml fresh parsley, hashed
- Salt and black pepper to taste

Instructions:

1. Flour, eggs, milk, and salt are mixed together in a dish using a whisk to create a batter that is smooth.
54. Start the cooking process by bringing a large pot of salted water to a boil.
55. Put the batter through a spaetzle machine or a colander, and then drop it into the water that is already boiling.
56. Cook the spaetzle for two to three mins, or until they rise to the surface of the water.
57. Butter should be melted in the pan, then garlic should be sautéed until it smells wonderful.
58. Once the spaetzle is done, add it to the skillet and mix it with the garlic butter to coat it.
59. Season.
60. Before serving, sprinkle the dish with freshly hashed parsley.

Nutrition: Kcals: 320 Protein: 10g Carbs: 50g Fat: 8g Fiber: 3g

45. Pretzel Dumplings with Beer Cheese Sauce

- Setup: 30mins
- Cook: 20mins
- Serves: 6

Ingredients:

- 500g pretzel rolls, cubed
- 3 eggs
- 250ml milk
- 1 onion, finely hashed
- 30g butter
- 300ml beer
- 200g sharp cheddar cheese, grated
- 30g flour
- Salt and black pepper to taste
- Hashed chives

Instructions:

1. Eggs and milk should be mixed together in a dish using a whisk.
61. The egg mixture should be poured over the pretzel rolls that have been cut into cubes and allowed to absorb the liquid.
62. In a frying pan, melt the butter and cook the onion after it has been finely hashed until it has softened.
63. After adding the beer, reduce the heat to a low simmer.
64. Grated sharp cheddar cheese and flour are gradually added while the mixture is stirred until it is smooth.
65. Season.
66. Construct the pretzel mixture into dumplings, then steam them for fifteen to twenty mins.
67. To serve, drizzle the dumplings with beer cheese sauce and top with hashed chives that have been hashed.

Nutrition: Kcals: 420 Protein: 15g Carbs: 35g Fat: 20g Fiber: 2g

46. German Potato Pancakes

- Setup: 15mins
- Cook: 20mins
- Serves: 4

Ingredients:

- 4 huge potatoes, peeled and grated
- 1 onion, grated
- 2 eggs
- 45g flour
- 5g baking powder
- 2.5g salt
- Oil for frying
- Sour cream and applesauce for serving

Instructions:

1. In a dish, combine the grated onion and potatoes that have been grated.
68. Squeeze off any extra liquid from the mixture by placing it on a clean kitchen towel and doing so.
69. Eggs, flour, baking powder, and salt should each be combined in their own dish and whisked together.
70. After the egg mixture has been combined, pour it over the potatoes and toss to combine.
71. Oil should be heated in a skillet over medium to high heat.
72. The potato batter should be dropped by spoonfuls into the hot oil, and the back of the spoon should be used to flatten the batter.
73. Fry in oil until both sides have a golden brown color.
74. Potato pancakes should be accompanied by sour cream and apple sauce when served.

Nutrition: Kcals: 280 Protein: 6g Carbs: 40g Fat: 10g Fiber: 3g

47. Red Cabbage Slaw with Apple

- Setup: 15mins
- Cook: 0mins
- Serves: 6

Ingredients:

- 1/2 red cabbage, thinly hashed
- 2 apples, julienned
- 1 carrot, grated
- 100ml apple cider vinegar
- 50ml olive oil
- 30g honey
- 5g caraway seeds
- Salt and black pepper to taste
- Hashed fresh parsley

Instructions:

1. Consolidate red cabbage that has been finely hashed, apples that have been julienned, and grated carrot in a large dish.
75. Mix together apple cider vinegar, olive oil, honey, and caraway seeds in a small dish. Season with salt and black pepper to taste.
76. After pouring the dressing over the cabbage mixture, toss it to evenly distribute the dressing.
77. Before serving, the slaw should be allowed to marinade for at least half an hour.
78. Prepared fresh parsley should be used as a garnish.

Nutrition: Kcals: 180 Protein: 2g Carbs: 25g Fat: 8g Fiber: 5g

48. Mulled Wine with Spices

- Setup: 10mins
- Cook: 20mins
- Serves: 6

Ingredients:

- 750 milliliters red wine
- 100 grams sugar
- 1 orange, hashed
- 1 lemon, hashed
- 6 cloves
- 3 cinnamon sticks
- 1 star anise
- 1 vanilla pod, split
- Orange zest

Instructions:

1. A reduction of wine and sugar was carried out in a saucepan. Stir constantly while heating on low until the sugar is completely dissolved.
2. Include some orange slices, some lemon slices, some cloves, some cinnamon sticks, some star anise, and a vanilla pod that has been split open.
3. Maintain a low boil for the next twenty mins.
4. The wine should be strained before being served warm with orange zest as a garnish.

Nutrition: Kcals: 180 Carbs: 20g Alcohol: 10g Fiber: 2g

49. Warm Apple Cider Punch

- Setup: 15mins
- Cook: 30mins
- Serves: 8

Ingredients:

- 1 liter apple cider
- 500 milliliters orange juice
- 60 milliliters honey
- 4 cinnamon sticks
- 1 teaspoon whole cloves
- 1 orange, hashed
- 1 lemon, hashed

Instructions:

1. Put the apple cider, orange juice, honey, cinnamon sticks, and whole cloves into a large pot and combine the ingredients.
79. Bring it up to a simmer over a moderate heat setting. Turn the heat down and let it simmer for half an hour.
80. The spices should be discarded once the punch has been strained.
81. Slices of orange and lemon should be added to the warm apple cider punch before serving.

Nutrition: Kcals: 120 Carbs: 30g Fat: 0g Fiber: 2g

50. Traditional German Coffee with a Twist

- Setup: 5mins
- Cook: 5mins
- Serves: 4

Ingredients:

- 960 milliliters strong brewed coffee
- 60 milliliters chocolate syrup
- 60 milliliters whipped cream
- 15 milliliters grated orange zest
- 15 grams sugar

Instructions:

1. Blend together one cup of strong brewed coffee and one tablespoon of chocolate syrup in each individual coffee cup.
82. Put a small amount of whipped cream in the center of each cup.
83. Orange zest, grated, should be sprinkled on top, and sugar should be added to taste.
84. Enjoy this unique spin on the classic coffee drink of Germany with a little stir.

Nutrition: Kcals: 40 Carbs: 7g Fat: 2g Protein: 0g

51. Elderflower Lemonade

- Setup: 10mins
- Serves: 4

Ingredients:

- 500 milliliters elderflower syrup
- 1 liter sparkling water
- 1 lemon, thinly hashed
- Ice cubes
- Freshmint leaves

Instructions:

1. Combine elderflower syrup with sparkling water in a large pitcher. The pitcher should be covered.
85. Add lemon that has been hashed very thinly and mix it gently.
86. After the glasses have been filled with ice, the elderflower lemonade should be poured into them.
87. Fresh mint leaves should be used as a garnish, and the dish should be served cold.

Nutrition: Kcals: 60 Carbs: 15g Fat: 0g Fiber: 0g

52. Quinoa and Vegetable Pilaf

- Setup: 15mins
- Cook: 20mins
- Serves: 4

Ingredients:

- 200 grams quinoa
- 480 milliliters vegetable broth
- 1 zucchini, hashed
- 1 red bell pepper, hashed
- 1 carrot, grated
- 60 grams frozen peas
- 30 milliliters olive oil
- 5 grams cumin
- 2.5 grams paprika
- Salt and black pepper to taste
- Fresh parsley

Instructions:

1. Using ice water, wash the quinoa thoroughly.
88. Combined quinoa and vegetable broth should be combined in a pot. Bring to a boil, then immediately drop the heat to low and continue to cook until the quinoa is done.
89. Hashed zucchini, red bell pepper, shredded carrot, and frozen peas should be sautéed in olive oil that has been heated in a frying pan.
90. Mix in the cumin, paprika, salt, and black pepper once the quinoa has been cooked.
91. Before serving, garnish with some fresh hashed parsley.

Nutrition: Kcals: 320 Protein: 8g Carbs: 55g Fat: 8g Fiber: 8g

53. Roasted Brussels Sprouts and Sweet Potato Medley

- Setup: 10mins
- Cook: 30mins
- Serves: 4

Ingredients:

- 500 grams Brussels sprouts, halved
- 500 grams sweet potatoes, hashed
- 30 milliliters olive oil
- 5 grams garlic powder
- 5 grams smoked paprika
- Salt and black pepper to taste
- 60 milliliters balsamic glaze
- Hashed pecans

Instructions:

1. Turn the oven temperature up to 200 degrees Celsius (fan oven 180 degrees Celsius).
92. In a dish, combine halved Brussels sprouts and sweet potatoes that have been hashed with olive oil, garlic powder, smoked paprika, salt, and black pepper. Toss to combine.
93. Place the vegetables in an even layer on a baking sheet and roast them for about half an hour, or until they are golden and crispy.
94. The roasted medley would be delicious with a balsamic glaze drizzled over it.
95. Before serving, garnish with pecans that have been hashed.

Nutrition: Kcals: 280 Protein: 5g Carbs: 45g Fat: 10g Fiber: 10g

54. Herbed Chicken and Vegetable Quinoa

- Setup: 20mins
- Cook: 25mins
- Serves: 4

Ingredients:

- 200 grams quinoa
- 480 milliliters chicken broth
- 500 grams boneless, skinless chicken breasts, hashed
- 1 zucchini, hashed
- 240 grams red onion, thinly hashed
- 1 bell pepper, hashed
- 30 milliliters olive oil
- 5 grams dried thyme
- 5 grams dried rosemary
- Salt and black pepper to taste
- Fresh lemon wedges

Instructions:

1. Using ice water, wash the quinoa thoroughly.
96. Combined quinoa and chicken broth should be combined in a pot. Bring to a boil, then immediately drop the heat to low and continue to cook until the quinoa is done.
97. Hashed chicken should be cooked in a skillet with heated olive oil until it is browned.
98. When the zucchini, red onion, and bell pepper are cooked through, add them to the skillet along with the hashed zucchini. Continue to sauté the vegetables until they are soft.
99. Mix in the quinoa that has been cooked, the dried thyme, the dried rosemary, the salt, and the black pepper.
100. To bring out the brightness of the lemon taste, serve with fresh lemon wedges.

Nutrition: Kcals: 380 Protein: 30g Carbs: 45g Fat: 10g Fiber: 6g

55. Mediterranean Chickpea Stew

- Setup: 15mins
- Cook: 30mins
- Serves: 6

Ingredients:

- 2 cans chickpeas, drained and rinsed (about 480 grams)
- 400 grams cherry tomatoes, halved
- 1 huge red onion, hashed (about 240 grams)
- 3 cloves garlic, hashed
- 30 milliliters olive oil
- 5 grams dried oregano
- 5 grams ground cumin
- 2.5 grams smoked paprika
- 480 milliliters vegetable broth
- Salt and black pepper to taste
- Fresh feta cheese

Instructions:

1. Hashed red onion and garlic should be cooked together in a pot with olive oil until the onion and garlic become tender.
101. Add cherry tomatoes that have been cut in half, chickpeas, dried oregano, ground cumin, smoked paprika, salt, and black pepper.
102. After pouring in the vegetable broth, reduce the heat to maintain a simmer. Cook for twenty to thirty mins.
103. If necessary, make adjustments to the seasoning.
104. Serve the Chickpea Stew from the Mediterranean hot, with crumbled feta on top as a garnish.

Nutrition: Kcals: 320 Protein: 12g Carbs: 50g Fat: 8g Fiber: 10g

56. Minestrone

- Serves 6

Ingredients

Vegetable packet

- 1 medium carrot, diced
- 1 stalk celery, diced
- 3 cloves garlic, hashed
- 1 large onion, diced
- 1 zucchini, halved lengthwise and hashed
- 150 grams green or yellow beans, snapped

Herb packet

- 1 bay leaf
- 4 sprigs of oregano
- 4 sprigs of thyme
- 1 sprig rosemary
- 3 sprigs parsley

Other ingredients

- 15 milliliters olive oil
- 480 milliliters vegetable stock
- 800 grams diced tomatoes with their juice (or the equivalent in fresh hashed tomatoes and juice)
- 10 grams sugar
- 200 grams small shell pasta
- 425 grams kidney or cannellini beans, drained
- Grated Parmesan, for serving

Instructions

1. At home, make the packages with the vegetables and herbs. Take into consideration that the fresh herbs will start to wilt within the first few days of your vacation, and plan to prepare this meal as soon as possible after you have arrived at your destination.

2. Warm the oil in a Dutch oven of 14 inches in diameter that has been placed over 22 coals. After adding the vegetables from the packet, heat them until they start to become more pliable.
3. Add the sugar, tomatoes, and stock to the pot.
4. After the mixture has reached a rolling boil, stir in the pasta and herbs. Simmer with the lid on for 15–20 mins, or until the spaghetti reaches the desired tenderness.
5. Take out the bay leaf and any herb stalks you find. Mix the beans into the mixture. Reheat everything, then sprinkle some Parmesan on top before serving.

57. Corn Chowder

- Serves 6

Ingredients

Vegetable packet

- 1 onion, diced
- 1 stalk celery, thinly hashed
- 1 small carrot, thinly hashed

Other ingredients

- 4–6 slices bacon, hashed
- 1 medium potato, diced
- 720 grams frozen corn
- 720 milliliters whole milk
- Salt and pepper to taste
- 120 grams instant mashed potato flakes
- 60 grams grated cheddar

Instructions

1. At home, put together the satchel of vegetables.
2. Cook the bacon by placing a Dutch oven with a diameter of 14 inches on 22 coals. It is not necessary to drain the grease.
3. After adding the vegetable packet, continue to cook the vegetables until they are pliable. Mix in the cubed potato, the corn, the milk, as well as some salt and pepper.
4. Bring the mixture to a boil, then reduce the heat to a simmer and cook for 15–20 mins.
5. After stirring in the potato flakes and cheddar, continue cooking for another three to five mins, until the mixture has thickened.

58. Squash Soup

- Serves 6

Ingredients

Vegetable packet

- 1440 grams butternut squash, peeled and diced
- 1 medium onion, diced

Other ingredients

- 60 grams butter
- 1 Granny Smith apple, peeled, cored, and hashed
- 1.9 liters vegetable stock
- 2.5 grams red pepper flakes
- Salt and pepper to taste
- 240 milliliters coconut milk

Instructions

1. To prepare the squash and onion at home, peel and dice them. Put it in a bag that can be sealed back up again.
2. After melting the butter in a Dutch oven measuring 14 inches and being placed over 22 briquettes, add the apple, onion, and squash to the pot. About 15 mins of cooking time with the mixture being stirred occasionally until it begins to brown.
3. Include the crushed red pepper flakes, vegetable stock, salt, and pepper in the dish.
4. Bring the mixture up to a simmer, and allow it to continue cooking until the pieces have reached the desired degree of softness. Stir it occasionally with a whisk, and remove it from the heat after it has reached a smooth consistency.
5. After stirring in the coconut milk, the dish can then be served.

59. Curried Lentil Soup

- Serves 4–6

Ingredients

Spice packet

- 15 milliliters curry powder
- 2.5 grams cinnamon
- 2.5 grams ground ginger
- 1 bay leaf

Other ingredients

- 285 grams red lentils
- 30 milliliters olive oil
- 150 grams small red onion, diced
- 6 grams garlic, hashed
- 710 milliliters vegetable broth or water
- 400 milliliters coconut milk
- 30 grams tomato paste
- 1 bunch spinach leaves

Instructions

1. When you get back to your house, blend the spices in a small jar or bag.
2. Warm the oil in a Dutch oven of 12 inches in diameter that has been placed over 20 briquettes. After adding the lentils and spice mixture, continue to heat the mixture while stirring fairly constantly until the lentils have developed a nutty flavor and are starting to turn brown.
3. After adding the garlic and red onion, continue to sauté them until they begin to soften.
4. Mix in the water or the broth made from vegetables. Bring the concoction up to a rolling boil.
5. Make sure that eight of the briquettes are placed under the pot, and that twenty are placed on the cover. Simmer for about half an hour, or until the lentils reach the desired

tenderness, turning them frequently to prevent sticking or burning. Take the bay leaf out of the dish.

6. Cook until the spinach is wilted and the coconut milk, tomato paste, and spinach have been heated through.

Conclusion

The goal of the "One-Pot Cookbook" is to serve as your conductor in life's culinary symphony by directing you down the path to the creation of tasty, stress-free meals in a way that is both harmonic and enjoyable. As we get closer to the end of this culinary journey, let's take a min to pause and think about some of the most important ideas, life lessons, and the overall melody that has been woven throughout the many chapters of this culinary companion.

This cookbook's purpose has been crystal clear from the very beginning: to help you rethink your relationship with the kitchen, to make the process of cooking easier, and to infuse your meals with a symphony of flavors—all from the convenience of a single pot. Those are the three main goals of this cookbook. Your path to mastering cooking with only one pot has consisted of an investigation into the aesthetic value of this method of preparation, an appreciation of the advantages it offers, and a step-by-step instruction manual on how to gather the necessary equipment and ingredients.

The capacity of one-pot cooking to transform the seemingly monotonous act of preparing a meal into an experience that is harmonious and full of taste is the beauty of this method of cooking. It's a gastronomic version of a symphony, with the many components interacting with one another to produce a harmony of flavors that is both straightforward and complex. One-pot cooking is an art form that celebrates the joy of creating without the burden of complexity. From the effortless simplicity that comes with using just one pot to the ingredient versatility that allows you to explore a myriad of flavors, one-pot cooking is an art form that embraces the joy of creating without the burden of complexity.

One-pot dinners are not only aesthetically pleasing, but they also provide a plethora of other benefits. The fact that they require little to no cleanup, are inexpensive, and save both time and money makes them more than just a sensible option; they are a way of life.

Cooking with only one pot encourages healthier eating habits, amplifies flavors, and simplifies the process of cooking, making it accessible to everyone, from the time-crunched professional looking for efficiency to the health-conscious individual yearning for nutritious meals that are also flavorful.

When embarking on a voyage of cooking with only one pot, it is essential to equip yourself with the appropriate tools and supplies. Each instrument and item plays a part in the creation of the culinary masterpieces that define one-pot cooking. This includes high-quality Dutch ovens, razor-sharp chef's knives, aromatic vegetables, and meats that can be used in a variety of ways. For the purpose of guaranteeing a smooth and risk-free experience when cooking, the focus has been placed on organization, correct handling, and the significance of regular maintenance.

Your road to become a one-pot cooking master has begun with the purchase of this cookbook and continues throughout your gastronomic trip. Just like any other voyage, this one has been filled with both exciting new discoveries and reassuringly familiar comforts. You've gained the ability to confidently traverse the kitchen, and you've come to appreciate the ease of one-pot cooking while appreciating the plethora of rich and varied tastes it provides to your table.

If the concept of cooking with only one pot could be summed up in a single tune, it would be the hum of contentment, the rhythm of effectiveness, and the harmony of tastes blending together in a tango of ease. All of these elements come together to form the essence of one-pot cooking. This handbook has served as the sheet music, directing you through the notes of soups and stews, the crescendo of casseroles, and the soothing hum of slow-cooked wonders as you make your way through the recipes. It has brought to light the concept that cooking does not have to be an intimidating symphony of chaos but rather can be an enjoyable musical experience in which one pot acts as the conductor of one's culinary destinies.

In the beginning, it was promised that your time spent in the kitchen would be made easier, that the anxiety that comes along with meal preparation would be reduced, and that a solution would be provided that would fit in effortlessly with the flow of your life. As we get to the end of this excursion into the world of cuisine, it is abundantly clear that this promise has been kept. The one-pot method has evolved as a solution, a key to unlocking a world of tastes with minimal work and maximum satisfaction. This method allows for greatest satisfaction while requiring the least amount of time.

Even in the midst of our busy lives, I want you to come away from the "One-Pot Cookbook" with the understanding that cooking can be an enjoyable and satisfying experience. This is the single most important thing I want you to learn from the book. It is an invitation to welcome the ease, savor the tastes, and rediscover the pleasure of preparing meals that not only satiate the needs of the body but also satisfy the desires of the heart.

Remember that you are not merely cooking when you enter into your kitchen, equipped with the knowledge and inspiration you have gained from these pages. Instead, you are conducting a symphony, orchestrating tastes, and producing culinary masterpieces with the ease of just one pot. The "One-Pot Cookbook" isn't just a book; it's your culinary companion, your guide to a world where cooking is a celebration, and where every meal is a note in the symphony of your life. This book isn't just a collection of recipes; it's your culinary friend. I wish for your home's kitchen to be filled with the harmonies of happiness, the scents of contentment, and the flavors that take the commonplace and turn it into the remarkable. Have fun in the kitchen!

Made in the USA
Las Vegas, NV
07 January 2025